Robert K. Edwards

DASH DIET COOKBOOK FOR BEGINNERS

1200 DAYS OF LOW-SODIUM DISHES THAT CAN HELP YOU TO REDUCE BLOOD PRESSURE AND BOOST HEALTH, WITHOUT GIVING UP TASTE. 30-DAY FOOD PLAN INCLUDED.

FULL-COLOR EDITION!

DISCLAIMER NOTICE

Part One

The Overview

If you enjoyed the book, please consider leaving a review on Amazon. You can do so simply by scanning the following QR code with your phone.

Thank you!

INTRODUCTION

$\mathcal{M}$ any people require medication to regulate their blood pressure. People with moderate hypertension may just require lifestyle modifications, such as switching to a better diet. However, for people who must take medicine to control their blood pressure, leading healthy lifestyles and eating well can help them take less medication overall. The heart must work harder to pump blood containing essential nutrients and oxygen throughout the body as a result of high blood pressure. The blood vessels' arteries thicken, get scarred, and lose their flexibility. Even while this process is a natural part of aging, those with high blood pressure experience it more quickly. The heart needs to work harder as the arteries stiffen, and the heart muscle becomes thicker, weaker, and less able to pump blood. High blood pressure can damage arteries, which can then affect the organs they serve. This kind of harm, for instance, can harm the heart, resulting in a heart attack, the brain, resulting in a stroke, or the kidneys, resulting in kidney failure.

Your risk of getting high blood pressure (hypertension) is influenced by what you consume. According to research, high blood pressure can be avoided—Lowering salt consumption is part of the Dietary Approaches to Stop Hypertension (DASH) eating plan, which aims to prevent and treat hypertension. A blood pressure reading of 140/90 mmHg or greater is considered high. Prehypertension is defined as blood pressure between 120/80 and 139/89 millimeters of mercury (mmHg), which is the standard unit of measurement for blood pressure. But if you follow these recommendations, high blood pressure can be avoided and reduced.

Follow a healthy dietary regimen that calls for low-sodium foods, such as DASH.

Uphold a healthy weight.

Engage in light exercise for at least 2 hours and 30 minutes every week.

Scientists have developed specialized dietary methods to assist lower blood pressure because nutrition is known to play a significant impact in the development of high blood pressure. The DASH diet, which was created to help people manage high blood pressure and lower their risk of developing heart disease, is discussed in this book.

WHAT IS DASH DIET

Dietary Approaches to Stop Hypertension, or DASH diet, is a healthy eating strategy created to assist lower blood pressure and enhance overall health. The diet places an emphasis on consuming complete, nutrient-dense foods such fruits, vegetables, whole grains, lean proteins, and low-fat dairy products while avoiding those that are heavy in saturated and trans fats, added sugars, and sodium. It has been demonstrated that the DASH diet lowers blood pressure and lowers the risk of heart disease, stroke, and other illnesses. Additionally, it is a flexible and balanced diet that can be altered to accommodate different dietary needs and tastes.

DASH DIET CONTAINING BOTH FRUITS AND VEGETABLES

The diet was developed as a result of studies showing that those who ate a plant-based diet, such as vegans and vegetarians, had much lower rates of high blood pressure.

Because of this, the DASH diet prioritizes fruits and vegetables while also including certain lean protein sources, such as chicken, fish, and legumes. Red meat, salt, added sugars, and fat are all restricted in the diet. The fact that this diet limits salt consumption, according to scientists, is one of the key reasons people with high blood pressure can benefit from it. The standard DASH diet regimen recommends consuming no more sodium than 1 teaspoon (2,300 mg) per day, which is in accordance with the majority of national recommendations. The version with less salt advises taking no more than 3/4 teaspoon (1,500 mg) of sodium each day. Fruits, vegetables, low-fat milk, whole grains, fish, chicken, legumes, and nuts are the foundation of the DASH diet. It advises cutting off red meat, added sugars in foods and beverages, and sodium. The diet is heart-healthy because it reduces the consumption of saturated and trans fats while boosting the consumption of potassium, magnesium, calcium, protein, and fiber—nutrients thought to help regulate blood pressure.

Adhering to the DASH Diet entails consuming a range of foods from different food groups that studies have shown to be good for heart health while avoiding others that have been proven to be unhealthy. Essential components include the following:

1. Veggies and fruits

2. Whole grain foods

3. Legumes, seeds, and nuts

4. Limit your intake of red and processed meat and focus on lean proteins like fish and chicken.

5. Fat-free or low-fat dairy

6. Avoid clear beverages with added sugar.

7. Low salt—if kept to fewer than 2,300 mg per day, the diet is much more beneficial for lowering blood pressure, which can fall to even lower levels with less than 1,500 mg per day of sodium intake.

8. Increased intake of dietary components such as fiber, calcium, magnesium, and potassium

9. Saturated fat, trans fat, and cholesterol levels that are lower

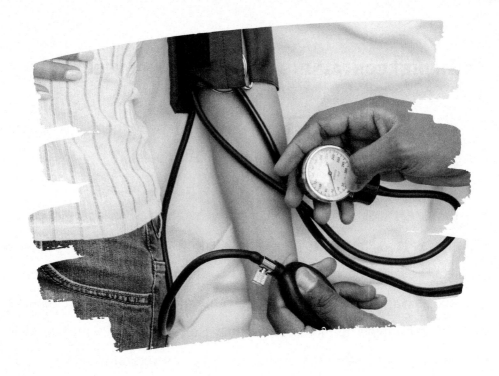

The Dietary Approaches to Stopping Hypertension (DASH) Diet is based on two studies that examined strategies to lower blood pressure through dietary changes, DASH and DASH-Sodium. In the DASH study, participants were given one of three diets: the DASH diet, which is high in fruits, vegetables, and low-fat dairy products and low in saturated fat, total fat, and cholesterol. The other two diets were similar to the typical North American diet in terms of nutrients. The findings were convincing. Both the DASH diet and the diet richer in fruits and vegetables lower blood pressure. Blood pressure was most significantly lowered by the DASH diet within two weeks of beginning the program. Total cholesterol as well as low-density lipoprotein (LDL), or "bad cholesterol," were decreased in addition to blood pressure. Participants in the DASH-Sodium study were randomly assigned to one of three sodium regimens: the DASH diet with 3,300 mg of sodium per day (a normal amount for many North Americans); 2,300 mg of sodium; or 1,500 mg of sodium (a more restricted amount, equivalent to about 2/3 of a teaspoon of salt); or no sodium at all. Every person on the DASH diet experienced decreased blood pressure. However, people's blood pressure decreased more significantly the less salt they ate. The highest drop in blood pressure was seen in those who previously had high blood pressure.

Numerous studies demonstrate the DASH diet's numerous health advantages. DASH lowers blood pressure in those with high blood pressure as well as in people with normal blood pressure, even without reducing sodium intake, according to a body of reliable evidence. If salt intake is restricted to less than 2300 mg per day, and even more so with a 1500 mg sodium restriction, it can result in significant blood pressure decreases.

DASH has also been shown to lower serum uric acid levels in people with hyperuricemia, which puts them at risk for a painful inflammatory condition known as gout. This is in comparison to a standard American diet (e.g., high intake of red and processed meats, beverages sweetened with sugar, sweets, and refined grains). DASH is best for enhancing all of these illnesses because persons with gout frequently also have high blood pressure and other cardiovascular diseases.

In a controlled 8-week trial, participants were randomly assigned to follow the DASH diet (low in total/saturated fat with whole grains, poultry, fish, nuts, fruits, and vegetables), a fruit and vegetable-rich diet (more fruits and vegetables than control diet but same amount of fat), or a control diet (the typical American diet, which is high in fat and cholesterol). The DASH diet was found to reduce cardiovascular risk. Based on the individuals' blood pressure and cholesterol readings before and after the diet intervention, the researchers calculated a 10-year reduction in risk for cardiovascular disease. Participants who followed the DASH or fruit/vegetable diets had a 10% lower risk than those who followed the control diet, although women and Black people exhibited the biggest advantages with a 13% and 14% risk reduction, respectively.

BRIEF HISTORY OF DASH DIET

In the US, high blood pressure is characterized as having a reading that is typically greater than 140/90 mmHg and affects one in three persons. The systolic pressure of blood against the arteries when the heart is contracting is represented by the top number, 140. The diastolic pressure in the arteries during rest or between heartbeats is represented by the bottom number, 90. The risk of heart disease, renal disease, and stroke increases with blood pressure, which is cause for alarm. Since high blood pressure has no symptoms or warning indications, it is referred to as the silent killer.

The National Heart, Lung, and Blood Institute's (NHLBI) DASH research was the first to examine the impact of a diet high in potassium, magnesium, and calcium—rather than supplements—on blood pressure. It was published in the New England Journal of Medicine in 1977.
459 adults with and without high blood pressure participated in the study.

Blood pressure levels needed to be between 80 and 95 mmHg for diastole and less than 160 mmHg for systole. 60% of the participants were African Americans, and around half of them were women. Three diets were contrasted. The first had a high fat content (37% of calories) and little fruit and vegetables, much like the usual American diet. The American diet was the second option, although it included more fruits and vegetables. The third diet had a high fruit and vegetable content, low-fat dairy products, and overall low fat content (less than 30% of calories). Per 2,000 calories, it also offered 1,240 mg calcium, 500 mg magnesium, and 4,700 mg potassium. The DASH diet is now referred to as this. Each of the three regimens had the same amount of sodium, or 7 grams (g) of salt, or around 3,000 mg of sodium per day. This was close to the current salt intake guidelines of 4-5 g per day and about 20% less than the average adult intake in the United States. Each person's calorie intake was modified to maintain weight. To rule out salt restriction and weight loss as probable causes for any changes in blood pressure, these two parameters were added. To improve adherence to the diets, all of the participants' meals were prepared in one large kitchen.

The DASH regimen was the most successful, according to the results, although eating more fruits and vegetables also had a lowering effect. It decreased systolic pressure by 6 mmHg and diastolic pressure by 3 mmHg in subjects without high blood pressure. Participants with high blood pressure had better outcomes; their systolic and diastolic pressures dropped by almost twice as much, to 11 and 6 mmHg, respectively. These findings demonstrated that the DASH diet appeared to drop blood pressure in a manner comparable to that found with the use of a single blood pressure medication, as well as a diet that restricted salt intake to 3 grams. The DASH plan's effects, which are equivalent to drug treatment, were felt after two weeks of beginning it and persisted throughout the course of the experiment. This trial offered the first scientific proof that dietary components other than sodium alone, such as potassium, calcium, and magnesium, had a significant impact on blood pressure.

MEDICAL SPECIALIZATIONS

In the 1990s, the DASH diet—an acronym for Dietary Approaches to Stop Hypertension—was created as a dietary strategy to lower hypertension combined with a decrease in dietary salt. The Mediterranean diet, which encourages a diet high in fruits and vegetables, low-fat dairy products, soluble dietary fiber, whole grains, and plant-based protein while being low in saturated fatty acids, serves as the main inspiration for this diet.

The authors draw attention to the high potassium content of this diet. The DASH diet is endorsed by the American Heart Association and is widely acknowledged by medical professionals as a useful method of controlling blood pressure. Thus, the DASH diet considerably lowers systolic and diastolic blood pressure in both hypertensive and normotensive individuals (by 11 and 5 mmHg, respectively), compared to a control diet, whose daily dose of table salt is already decreased to 8 grams. The DASH diet is today regarded as one of the best diets for sustaining good health, in accordance with the recommendations of public health authorities, in addition to its effects on cardiovascular health.

The MIND diet was created by the team of Martha Claire Morris, who released the initial findings in 2015. The moniker MIND, an acronym for Mediterranean-DASH Intervention for Neurodegenerative Delay, refers to a diet that is likewise based on the principles of the Mediterranean diet and builds on the DASH diet by providing a prominent place to items and ingredients that may enhance brain health. Green vegetables (spinach, lettuce, green beans) and other vegetables, nuts (walnuts, hazelnuts, almonds), berries (raspberries, currants, blueberries), dried beans, whole grains, fish and poultry (occasionally), olive oil, and even wine—in moderation—are among the ten foods recommended by the MIND diet. On the other hand, this approach suggests limiting the consumption of five food categories: red meats, butter and fatty cheeses, pastries, and fried meals. It is therefore advised not to eat more than four portions of red meat or even five pastries per week, which is a limitation but not a ban. This gives one some latitude to sample their preferred meals without getting too frustrated.

Both for sustaining good mental health and as a method of preserving good general health, this MIND diet exhibits some encouraging results. To confirm the beneficial effects of this diet with greater assurance, large-scale, long-term research will be required.

The DASH and MIND diets, like the Mediterranean diet, are very simple to follow and have lower dropout rates than diets that are more restrictive or demand significant behavioral adjustments.

There are no nutrient categories that are prohibited by the DASH, MIND, or Mediterranean diets. They approach international nutritional requirements by recommending various sources and adjusting the ratios.

Therefore, unlike other diets that promote or strongly restrict one of the groups, these diets always allow for starchy meals (carbohydrates that are broken down into sugars), proteins, and lipids. Thus, the proportion of starches and lipids in the Dukan and Atkins diets was dramatically reduced in favor of proteins, while the Paleolithic diet severely limited carbs in favor of lipids and proteins. Although such imbalances can have positive short-term impacts, particularly on weight loss, the scientific community strongly doubts their long-term implications.

THE MEDITERRANEAN DIET AND
THE DASH DIET SHARE FIVE GUIDING PRINCIPLES

The main principles of the Mediterranean diet serve as inspiration for other DASH diet principles. Let's start by pointing out that both lead to a simpler, healthier, and more diversified diet.

1 -- Fruits and vegetables at the heart of the diet

Consuming foods that are naturally low in sodium, or favoring fresh fruits and vegetables, is one of the tenets of the DASH diet. They also serve as our primary supply of fiber and are a good source of vitamins, minerals, trace elements, and antioxidants, which is a plus.

Also worth remembering is the superior design of nature. The reason why fruits and vegetables are in season is that they give us the nutrients we require at the appropriate time. For example, the bulk of summertime fruits and vegetables are mostly water to help us stay hydrated throughout the dry and hot weather.

How about in terms of volume? The Mediterranean diet advises eating a serving of vegetables with each meal. The DASH diet presents a greater challenge because everything depends on calorie intake and profile. However, the amount varies daily between 300 and 400 g (80 to 100 g is about similar to one portion). that is, three to four pieces each day.

2 -- No to processed products

As we've seen, one of the DASH diet's tenets is to limit foods that are heavy in sodium, oil, and saturated sugars. To limit intake of prepared meals, processed foods, and fried foods in particular.

In order to benefit from fresh, uncooked foods, the DASH diet emphasizes them more than the Mediterranean diet does. The DASH diet is a return to the fundamentals. To concentrate on the best components of the other food groups (including fruits and vegetables), remove the extraneous ingredients from prepared meals.

3 -- More legumes, dried fruits and whole grains on the menu

Regarding additional food groups, here are three that are becoming less and less common in our kitchens but still play a role in these two diets: legumes (like chickpeas and lentils), dry fruits (like pecans and walnuts), and whole grains (like whole wheat pasta or even quinoa, brown rice, and corn).

Including them in our diets not only adds diversity but also offers their beneficial nutrients.

Additionally, by combining legumes and whole grains, we can increase our intake of protein while decreasing our consumption of animal proteins, particularly red meat. Additionally, this combo offers fiber and complex carbohydrates.

4 -- Less salt and more spices to cook differently

In the modern kitchen, salt is widely used. It replaces the primary (or even special) taste enhancer. It is not the only component that can fulfill this function, though. Mediterranean's use spices, herbs, and garden herbs in their daily cooking. They provide the food flavor and make it possible to change up the recipes.

If the same pan-fried vegetables are prepared with basil, coriander, mint, saffron, or turmeric, they will have various fragrances, benefits, and flavors.

The aim is to cook differently whether you choose to follow the DASH diet or the Mediterranean diet. cooking with different condiments once more. Use fresh or dried herbs and spices, as well as garlic, onion, and less salt.

5 -- Regular physical activity

The DASH diet also suggests engaging in regular physical activity. The idea is not necessarily to go into a sport or to do it intensely, like in Mediterranean culture. Simply go for a stroll, swim, or get some fresh air. It's important to move.

Speaking of basics, other key components of the Mediterranean diet include laughing, grinning, taking deep breaths, and appreciating the surroundings. Because the Mediterranean diet teaches us how to live well, whereas the DASH diet teaches us the fundamentals of (excellent) nutrition!

THE HEALTH BENEFITS
OF THE DASH DIET

*T*he DASH diet is a whole foods regimen that emphasizes the consumption of fresh produce, whole grains, legumes, nuts, low-fat dairy products, fish, and chicken. Being naturally low in sodium, refined sugar, and saturated and trans fats, it is regarded as a heart-healthy diet. It improves the intake of fiber, antioxidants, potassium, magnesium, calcium, and other nutrients that are crucial for cardiovascular health. The DASH diet and continued physical activity will have the biggest impact on decreasing blood pressure and some other benefit to the health system which include Reduce High Blood Pressure.

Blood arteries experience pressure when blood flows through them, and this pressure is measured as blood pressure. Systolic pressure over diastolic pressure, or 120/80 mmHg, is how blood pressure is measured in millimeters of mercury (mmHg). The top number, or systolic blood pressure, represents the pressure in the veins when the heart beats. The pressure in the vessels while the heart is not beating is known as diastolic blood pressure, which is represented by the bottom number.

Following are the categories used by the American College of Cardiology to categorize blood pressure:

·More than 120/80 mmHg is abnormal.

·Diastolic less than 80 mmHg and systolic 120-129 mmHg are considered elevated.

·Systolic 130-139 mmHg or diastolic 80-89 mmHg is stage 1 hypertension.

·Systolic 140 mmHg or diastolic 90 mmHg is considered stage 2 hypertension.

·Systolic pressure of 180 mmHg or higher and/or a diastolic pressure of 120 mmHg constitute a hypertensive crisis.

Systolic pressure: The force exerted by your heartbeat on your blood vessels.

Diastolic pressure: When your heart is at rest, this is the pressure in your blood arteries between beats.

Blood pressure increases can also be caused by genes and stress. Your doctor can occasionally be unable to pinpoint a specific cause for your high blood pressure. What is described as essential hypertension is that. When your doctor discusses your blood pressure with you, he is talking to the force that your blood exerts on the artery walls. Your systolic blood pressure is the highest reading on the scale. That pressure is the result of your heart's pumping action on your blood vessels. The diastolic blood pressure, which is shown by the lower figure, is the pressure experienced while your heart is at rest in between beats. Your blood pressure should remain 120 over 80 or below. High blood pressure is defined as 140 over 90 or higher.

You might wonder why high blood pressure is a concern. High blood pressure might be compared to a river that is flowing too quickly; eventually, the banks will be damaged. When you have high blood pressure, your artery walls gradually become damaged due to the additional pressure your blood exerts on them. Additionally, it can harm your kidneys, heart, and other organs. How can you determine if you have high blood pressure, then? Because high blood pressure frequently lacks signs like a fever or a cough, you may not even be aware of it. The majority of the time, high blood pressure has no symptoms at all, and you won't know you have it unless you've had it checked or you've experienced complications like heart disease or renal issues. You can use a home blood pressure monitor to check it yourself, or you can visit your doctor to have it done. If it's high, you'll decide on a blood pressure target with your doctor. You can accomplish that objective by following a balanced diet, doing out for at least 30 minutes each day, giving up smoking, consuming less than 1,500 milligrams of salt each day, and employing stress-relieving techniques like yoga and meditation. If, however, these lifestyle modifications are insufficient to control your blood pressure, your doctor may recommend one or more medications.

Because uncontrolled blood pressure can lead to a number of significant health issues, including as heart attack, stroke, renal disease, and eyesight loss, doctors take their patients' blood pressure very seriously. It's better to take control of your blood pressure by being proactive. The DASH diet has its roots in the 1990s, when the NIH supported multiple research to identify a therapeutic diet that was successful in treating high blood pressure. They came to the conclusion that blood pressure might be lowered by the DASH diet without weight reduction or purposeful sodium restriction. Blood pressure reductions can be amplified by using the DASH diet in conjunction with sodium control and weight loss.

REDUCE HIGH CHOLESTEROL

What is cholesterol?

A lipid (fat) called cholesterol is produced by the liver and is present in many of the foods we consume. Cholesterol is necessary for good health because it performs various crucial tasks for the efficient operation of your body.

·The membranes of your cells absorb about 90% of the cholesterol in your body.

·It functions as a component of specific sex hormones (testosterone) or adrenal hormones (cortisone).

·It controls how specific fetal cells develop.

·It encourages the development of synapses in the brain.

·It is a component of bile, a fluid that digests dietary fats by combining lipids and water.

·It is a form of vitamin D.

LDL (Low Density Lipoprotein), a low-density protein, and HDL (High Density Lipoprotein), a high-density lipoprotein, are two types of "lipoproteins" that transport cholesterol in the blood. The terms "total cholesterol" refer to both HDL and LDL cholesterol, also known as good (HDL) and bad (LDL) cholesterol.

The good cholesterol: When cholesterol builds up in the arteries, HDL lipoproteins pick it up and carry it to the liver, where it is excreted. Poor-quality fatty deposits are removed from the arteries by HDL cholesterol. HDL binds 20–30% of blood cholesterol.

Bad cholesterol: LDL lipoproteins, which are bad for the body, bind cholesterol to the artery walls and cause atherosclerotic plaques to develop. Since LDL makes up 60 to 80% of the cholesterol in the blood, it has a tendency to clog the arteries.

It is a necessary component not only for the construction of the membrane that envelops the cells but also for the manufacture of several hormones. Although high cholesterol is a risk factor for various heart and blood vessel illnesses, it is not a disease in and of itself. After numerous years of having too much cholesterol, the arteries gradually lose their flexibility, which reduces their diameter. This condition is known as atherosclerosis (also known as arteriosclerosis), a condition with potentially harmful effects.

The treatment of excess cholesterol is based on dietary measures and specific medications. Although high cholesterol is a risk factor for various heart and blood vessel illnesses, it is not a disease in and of itself. In actuality, an excess of LDL cholesterol, often known as bad cholesterol, encourages the development of deposits on the artery walls. These buildups gradually limit the diameter of the arteries and induce a loss of flexibility in the arteries, which raises the risk of infarction, stroke, or arteritis.

Effect and Symptoms of High Cholesterol

Although high LDL cholesterol does not directly result in disease, its buildup in the arteries can. For instance, myocardial infarction, angina pectoris, or even a heart artery contraction. Paralysis, vertigo, linguistic difficulties, and even a stroke may result from clogged brain arteries. Arteritis results in sporadic calf cramps during walking if the arteries in the legs are restricted. Additionally, erectile dysfunction is noted.

How Dash Diet Reduce High Cholesterol

The DASH diet includes a number of elements that have been shown to lower cholesterol levels, including eating a lot of fiber (which comes from fruits, vegetables, whole grains, nuts, and legumes), eating fish and leaner meat cuts, and avoiding sugar and refined carbohydrates. However, the DASH diet also causes a reduction in HDL ("good") cholesterol. The DASH diet is helpful at lowering markers of LDL and VLDL ("bad") cholesterol and triglycerides. Further studies have revealed that a higher fat DASH diet, which replaces 10% of the total daily calories from carbohydrates with unsaturated fat, is equally as effective at lowering blood pressure, LDL cholesterol, and triglycerides without causing unintended decreases in HDL cholesterol.

REDUCE CARDIOVASCULAR DISEASES

Heart and blood vessel illnesses are collectively referred to as cardiovascular diseases. These conditions may impact a single or multiple areas of your heart and/or blood vessels. A person may have symptoms (physical manifestations of the disease) or be asymptomatic (complete lack of symptoms).

Cardiovascular disease encompasses problems with the heart or blood vessels, such as:

- Narrowing of the blood arteries in your body, whether it be in your heart, other organs, or elsewhere.
- Birth defects in the heart and blood vessels are evident.
- improperly functioning heart valves.
- abnormal heartbeats.

Depending on the exact form, cardiovascular disease can have a variety of causes. For instance, coronary artery disease and peripheral artery disease are brought on by atherosclerosis (plaque buildup in your arteries). Arrhythmias can be brought on by coronary artery disease, cardiac muscle scarring, genetic issues, or drug side effects. Valve problems can be brought on by aging, infections, an improper diet, and rheumatic disease.

What are the risk factors for cardiovascular disease?

If you have risk factors like these, you could be more prone to develop cardiovascular disease:

·Hypertension is a term for high blood pressure.

·Hyperlipidemia, or high cholesterol.

·Use of tobacco, including vaping.

·Diabetes type 2.

·Heart disease in the family history.

·Absence of exercise.

·Being overweight or obese.

·Diet high in sodium, sugar and fat.

·Alcoholism in excess.

·Use of illegal or prescription drugs.

·Gestational diabetes.

·Chronic inflammatory or autoimmune conditions.

·Chronic kidney disease.

Depending on the reason, cardiovascular disease symptoms can change. More modest symptoms may be seen in older folks and those who were born assigned as females.

They are still susceptible to major cardiovascular disease, though.

Signs of a cardiac condition:

- Angina, or chest pain.
- Pressure, weight, or discomfort in the chest that has been compared to a "belt around the chest" or a "weight on the chest."
- Dyspnea, or shortness of breath.
- fainting or dizziness.
- weariness or fatigue.

HOW DASH DIET REDUCE CARDIOVASCULAR DISEASES

Adopting the DASH (Dietary Approaches to Stop Hypertension) diet may have the biggest impact on young and middle-aged persons among numerous lifestyle changes that may lower cardiovascular disease. Over the next ten years, researchers predict that broad adoption of lifestyle modifications, such as avoiding excessive alcohol intake and engaging in regular exercise, might avert thousands of deaths and save more than $1 billion in medical expenses. According to their findings, following the DASH diet could be most advantageous.

The DASH diet is especially created to assist in controlling blood pressure. The diet places a strong emphasis on foods including fruits, vegetables, lean meat sources, nuts, seeds, and whole grains while restricting the consumption of red meat, sodium, sweets, and beverages with added sugar. The majority of cardiovascular disorders, such as heart attack and stroke, are significantly influenced by hypertension. The DASH diet can effectively lower and normalize blood pressure, which can dramatically reduce the risk of cardiovascular disease by 20%. It is specifically linked to a 29% lower risk of heart failure and a 19% lower risk of stroke.

WEIGHT LOSS

The DASH diet is an effective option for managing weight, especially for those who are overweight or obese. According to a recent meta-analysis, persons who followed the DASH diet for 24 weeks lost more weight than those who followed a calorie-restricted conventional American diet.

Whether or not you lose weight while following the DASH diet, you'll probably have decreased blood pressure. However, it's likely that you have received advice to decrease weight if you already have high blood pressure.

This is because your blood pressure is more likely to be greater the more weight you have. Additionally, it has been demonstrated that decreasing weight can lower blood pressure. According to certain research, the DASH diet can help people lose weight.

Those who have lost weight on the DASH diet, on the other hand, have done so while maintaining a regulated calorie deficit, which means they were instructed to consume fewer calories than they were burning. People may discover that they automatically cut back on their calorie consumption and lose weight when following the DASH diet since it excludes so many high-fat, sugary meals. Others might need to consciously limit their intake. In either case, you'll still need to follow a calorie-reduced diet if you wish to lose weight while following the DASH diet.

DASH has proven to work. If you want to lose weight, DASH won't help you do so quickly. However, it is possible to lose weight and improve your health at the same time if you choose the right calorie amount and keep to it consistently. There are numerous free web resources available to get assistance because DASH has been used for so long and is widely regarded by medical professionals.

REDUCE TYPE 2 DIABETES

A 20% risk decrease in developing type 2 diabetes in the future is linked to the DASH diet. Diabetes type 2 and prediabetes are preceded by insulin resistance, which is the body's desensitization to insulin and the rise in blood sugar that results. The DASH diet successfully raises insulin sensitivity, especially when used in conjunction with a complete program for lifestyle modification that involves exercise and weight loss. Weirdly, both high- and low-GI DASH diets had the same effects on insulin sensitivity, suggesting that using the glycemic index (GI) to choose foods high in carbohydrates is not necessary.

Enhance the Metabolic Syndrome

High blood pressure, high blood sugar, abdominal obesity, low HDL cholesterol, and high triglycerides are at least three of the symptoms of metabolic syndrome. The DASH diet can help manage and prevent metabolic syndrome by enhancing these indicators.

Lower Your Gout Risk

DASH can lower serum uric acid levels in comparison to a Standard American Diet, which reduces the risk of gout. The DASH diet would be beneficial in treating all problems given that it is widely believed that gout is a metabolic disease that frequently co-occurs with high blood pressure and other cardiovascular disorders.

Improve Kidney Health

A lower risk of kidney disease is linked to DASH dietary patterns, which include consuming less red meat and processed food and more nuts, legumes, and low-fat dairy products. The DASH diet's high consumption of calcium, phytates, magnesium, and citrate is linked to a lower incidence of kidney stones, as does consuming fruits and vegetables.

THE DASH DIET FOOD

*S*imilar to the well-known Mediterranean diet, the Dash diet prioritizes "good" fats, lean animal proteins, water, soluble and insoluble fibers, vitamins, minerals, antioxidants (flavonoids, polyphenols...), and vegetable proteins. Specifically, humans ingest 27% fats, 18% proteins, and 55% carbohydrates everyday.

Here are some reminders to "eat Dash" without making your life more difficult:

- We eat 5 portions of 80 g each of fresh or frozen fruits and vegetables, without added sugar, at the rate of 3 fruits and 2 vegetables each day.
- We eat a portion of meat, an egg, fish, seafood, tofu, or a vegetarian steak every day at noon and in the evening.
- We eat a little amount of potatoes, whole grains, or other starchy foods at every meal.
- We consume a minimum of 1 liter of water every day, or 75% water and 25% tea or herbal tea.

The best Dash foods are thus:

1.Garlic: This detox food boosts the immune system's function and helps maintain a healthy balance of intestinal flora in addition to being great for the heart (anti-cholesterol, anti-hypertension, etc.). Additionally, it has a healthy amount of prebiotic fibers (1 gram for 2 raw pods) that nourish the "good" bacteria that live in our intestines.

2.Berries: Blueberries, blackberries, currants, blackcurrants, and other small red and black fruits are extremely low in calories and sugar; these are without a doubt the greatest "Dash" fruits because they are also extremely concentrated in vitamins, minerals, and antioxidants.

3.Broccoli: For the liver, intestinal flora, heart, brain, and immunity, broccoli is a fantastic source of vitamin C, calcium, and protective phytochemicals. This is true of all cabbages: It must be, whether it is uncooked, cooked, fresh, or frozen.

4.Turmeric: A super-joke from Dash: Turmeric lowers cholesterol and reduces inflammation. Additionally, it treats intestinal issues with nearly no calories.

5.Sardines: Sardines, like all fish, are a great option for a Dash plate that is well-balanced. It also has a good amount of vitamin D and omega-3 fatty acids without being overly polluted.

FRUIT

4 to 5 servings are recommended per day.

The DASH diet permits the consumption of all fruits. In fact, it encourages their consumption, dismissing concerns about the natural sugars in fruits being unhealthy. Enjoy 4 to 5 servings daily, incorporating them into desserts, toppings, smoothies, and snacks. Each person should be served with just 1/2 cup of fresh fruit and 1/4 cup of dried fruit. Here's a revised list of fruit examples: Apples, Blueberries, Grapes, Kiwi, Oranges, Raspberries, Banana, Peach, Pear, Nectarine, Plum, Cherries, Berries, Mango, Pineapple, Melon Strawberries

LOW-FAT DAIRY PRODUCTS

2-3 servings every day.

Replace your full-fat dairy products with low-fat or fat-free options since the diet advises avoiding foods high in saturated fat. However, you can still have 2 to 3 servings of dairy products daily, as long as they are low in fat and sodium. Here's a revised list of dairy products: Cheese, Eggs, Low fat yogurt, Milk, Yogurt

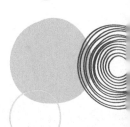

HIGH-SODIUM FOODS

4 to 5 servings are recommended per day.

The DASH diet permits the consumption of all fruits. In fact, consuming them is encouraged by the diet. Get over your concern that fruit's inherent sugars are unhealthy. Enjoy 4 to 5 servings daily in the form of dessert, toppings, smoothies, and snacks. Just 1/2 cup of fresh fruit and 1/4 cup of dried fruit should be served per person.

Apples, Blueberries, Grapes, Kiwi, Oranges, Raspberries, Banana, Peach, Pear, Nectarine, Plum, Cherries, Berries, Mango, Pineapple, Melon Strawberries

LEAN PROTEINS

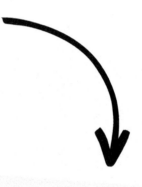

Although the vegetarian lifestyle served as the inspiration for the DASH diet, it is not entirely plant-based. A maximum of 6 ounces of lean meat or eggs may be consumed per day. Although it may not seem like much, persons with hypertension and heart health issues may benefit from eating less meat. Steer clear of frying and stick to poultry and fish. Tofu and tempeh are options for vegetarians and vegans.

Chicken, oily fish, Herrings, Mackerel, Salmon, Sardines, Tuna, lean beef, Turkey

VEGETABLES

5 to 6 servings should be consumed daily.Vegetables are a beloved food category for many people. As you age, vegetables become even more appealing. The DASH diet recommends consuming five to six servings of vegetables per day. Don't be afraid to explore new vegetables like spaghetti squash, but also consider using familiar favorites like peas and carrots in soups, salads, and side dishes.

Here is a list of vegetables that you can incorporate into your diet: chickpeas, black beans, black-eyed peas, red beans, potatoes, sweet potatoes, avocados, peppers, carrots, cucumbers, garlic, kale, lettuce, onions, seeds, chia seeds, flaxseed, pumpkin, sunflower, spinach, tomatoes, and zucchini

GRAINS AND STARCHY FOODS

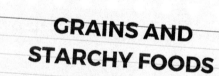

Servings per day: 6 to 8
The DASH diet emphasizes the consumption of whole grains due to their ability to lower the risk of hypertension, with a recommended intake of 6 to 8 servings per day. While it may seem complicated, incorporating whole grains into your diet can be as simple as having whole grain cereal or oatmeal for breakfast, and choosing options like quinoa, brown rice, or whole wheat pasta for lunch and dinner.
Here is a list of foods that fall under the category of whole grains: sliced bread, tortillas, rolls, bagels, crackers (low sodium), dry cereal and granola, rice, pasta, quinoa, oats, grits, polenta, barley, couscous, ancient grains, sprouted grains, corn, lima beans, and yams

NUTS, SEEDS, BEANS, AND LEGUMES

4-5 servings each week.
This food group should be consumed four to five times per week, according to the DASH Diet. While legumes like beans and lentils are fantastic sources of plant protein and high in fiber, nuts and seeds are excellent sources of healthful fats. These high-fiber meals will help you increase your fiber intake, which is a key component of the DASH diet. All of these foods are rich in essential vitamins and minerals. However, due to their higher calorie content, the recommended servings for these food groups are fewer compared to other dietary groups. Almonds (unsalted), Pistachios (unsalted), Cashews (unsalted), Walnuts (unsalted), Peanuts (unsalted), Peanut Butter, Almond Butter, Tahini, Chia Seeds, Flax Seeds, Hemp Seeds, Sunflower Seeds, Sesame Seeds, Green Beans, Lentils

HEART-HEALTHY OILS

Servings: two to three per day
The Mediterranean diet, which is rich in healthful fats, served as inspiration for some aspects of the DASH diet. The DASH diet includes heart-healthy fats as well, which is why adherents eat 2 to 3 servings of monounsaturated fats daily. Olive oil will probably be your go-to oil.

- Olive oil
- Canola oil
- Safflower oil
- Low-fat mayonnaise

LOW FAT SWEETS

Although the designers of the DASH diet are aware that occasionally you'll want to reward yourself, it better to limit your consumption of sweets. In such situations, they have provided a list of sweets that are acceptable to consume five times a week or less.

The DASH diet endorses low-fat desserts include:

- Fruit-flavored gelatin
- Jelly
- Maple syrup
- Sorbet and ices

Seeds/cereals: Brown rice, Buckwheat, Bulgur, couscous, Pearl barley, Wholemeal pasta, Whole wheat bread

Foods and drinks to be avoided while following a DASH diet

The DASH diet is a balanced eating plan that does not eliminate any food groups, so it is not particularly novel. The DASH diet promotes the consumption of simple, natural foods that are free from chemical and industrial ingredients as much as possible. It shares similarities with the Mediterranean, Okinawa, and GI diets

RED MEATS

The DASH diet prioritizes fish and poultry over red meat, according to research conducted in 1999. Red meat consumption should be limited, although it is not technically forbidden, due to its high content of saturated fat and cholesterol. Red meats include:

- beef
- pork
- lamb
- veal

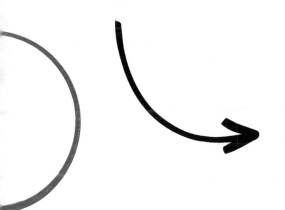

SATURATED FAT

There is conflicting data regarding the connection between saturated fat and heart disease; however, the DASH diet takes a cautious approach and advises reducing the consumption of foods high in saturated fat.

- Cheese
- Fatty cuts of meat
- Poultry with skin
- Lard
- Cream
- Butter
- Whole milk

ADDED SUGAR

You should become accustomed to reading the ingredient lists on packaged foods if you follow the DASH diet and avoid adding sugar cubes to your tea. Despite the limited research on sugar and hypertension, some data suggest that sugar may raise blood pressure. Even if there may not be a clear connection between the two, it is still advisable to limit added sugar because it is calorie-dense without providing any nutritional benefits.

- Table sugar
- Sweets
- Condiments with added sugar
- Junk food

You eat moderate portions of:

- Fat-free or low-fat dairy products. ·Whole grains. Lean meats, poultry, beans, soy foods, legumes, and eggs or egg substitutes
- Fish
- ·Nuts and seeds
- Heart-healthy fats, such as olive oil, canola oil, or avocados

FREQUENTLY ASKED QUESTIONS

QUESTION: Can Dash diet be vegetarian?

The DASH diet could easily be a vegetarian diet if legumes (for example, beans, lentils, peas, and peanuts) were substituted for meat. Vegetarian diets tend to be higher in potassium, magnesium, and calcium, as does the DASH diet. Vegetarian diets also are higher in fiber and unsaturated fats than other diets.

QUESTION: I can't tolerate lactose or am allergic to dairy. Can I still follow the DASH diet?

Yogurt, most cheeses, and warm milk products can all be consumed by lactose intolerant individuals in large quantities. Since nonfat milk still includes lactose, not sure why so many people can tolerate it. Additionally, some people who are allergic to or intolerant to milk proteins can consume yogurt or cheese. You can also use dairy alternatives like soy or rice milk, yogurt, or cheeses, as long as they have the same amounts of calcium and vitamin D as the original items. For those who are sensitive to the protein in cow's milk, goat milk is an additional option.

QUESTION: Is the DASH diet high fiber and low fat?

Yes, the DASH diet has a high fiber content and has little to no fat, most of which are heart-healthy fats. Extremely low-fat diets are linked to increased appetite, which is detrimental when trying to establish and maintain a balanced eating routine.

QUESTION: Is sea salt preferable to table salt for lowering sodium levels?

Although many varieties of sea salt have a little less sodium than ordinary salt, they can nevertheless contribute to high dietary sodium levels.

Additionally, sea salt frequently has smaller granules with higher weights (and sodium) per teaspoon. Instead of trying to rely just on adding salt to dishes to impart flavor, it is tremendously beneficial to learn various methods of seasoning. We encourage cooking with little to no extra salt in the DASH Diet Cookbook as well as in all of the recipes.

QUESTION: Can sweeteners be used in the DASH diet?

In the DASH diet, there is no specific mention of the use of artificial sweeteners. While artificial sweeteners can provide a low-calorie alternative for sweetening foods and beverages, it is important to consider that excessive use of artificial sweeteners may impact taste preferences for natural flavors. Additionally, some research suggests that excessive use of artificial sweeteners may be associated with metabolic issues and other health complications.

If you need to sweeten foods or beverages in the DASH diet, it is preferable to opt for more natural options such as fresh fruit, honey, or small amounts of cane sugar.

QUESTION: Is it recommended to skip breakfast?

No, it is not recommended to skip breakfast on the DASH diet. Breakfast is considered an important meal and an integral part of a healthy lifestyle.

Skipping breakfast may lead to feelings of hunger and a higher likelihood of making less healthy food choices throughout the rest of the day. Therefore, it is advisable to have a balanced breakfast as part of a healthy lifestyle based on the DASH diet.

QUESTION: What is the recommended duration for following the DASH diet?

The recommended duration for following the DASH diet depends on individual needs and goals. In general, the DASH diet is designed as a long-term dietary approach rather than a temporary diet.

However, every individual is different, so it is always advisable to consult a healthcare professional or a dietitian to obtain personalized guidance on the duration and adaptation of the DASH diet based on your specific needs and goals.

QUESTION: What can I do to prepare adequately before starting this diet?

Before starting the diet, you can prepare by educating yourself about the principles and guidelines of the DASH diet, stocking up on nutritious foods, and planning your meals and snacks in advance.

QUESTION: What are the tips for staying motivated and overcoming any challenges during this diet?

To stay motivated during the DASH diet, set realistic goals, track your progress, seek support from friends or family, find enjoyable ways to stay physically active, and remind yourself of the health benefits you will gain from following the diet.

QUESTION: What are the success strategies reported by others who have followed this diet?

Certain tactics for success have been shared by people who have followed the DASH diet. These include introducing dietary changes gradually, prioritizing whole and unprocessed foods, practicing portion control, decreasing sodium intake, and seeking personalized advice from healthcare professionals or registered dietitians.

Please be aware that these responses are concise, and for more comprehensive information, it is advisable to consult a healthcare professional or registered dietitian.

PLEASE NOTE THAT THESE ARE BRIEF RESPONSES, AND FOR
MORE DETAILED INFORMATION, IT IS RECOMMENDED
TO CONSULT A HEALTHCARE PROFESSIONAL OR REGISTERED DIETITIAN.

The recipe images are purely illustrative and represent a form of preparation and presentation that the reader can customize to their liking.

I recommend experimenting and letting your imagination runs wild, the best ingredient!

BUON APPETITO!

Part Two

The Recipes

Breakfast

1 SERVING

DIFFICULT

COST

BERRY-ALMOND SMOOTHIE BOWL

INGREDIENTS

- ⅔ cup frozen raspberries
- ½ cup frozen sliced banana
- ½ cup plain unsweetened almond milk
- 5 tablespoons sliced almonds, divided
- ¼ teaspoon ground cinnamon
- ⅛ teaspoon ground cardamom
- ⅛ teaspoon vanilla extract
- ¼ cup blueberries
- 1 tablespoon unsweetened coconut flakes

PREPARATION

1. Blend the following ingredients in a blender: raspberries, banana, almond milk, 3 tablespoons almonds, cinnamon, cardamom, and vanilla. Blend until extremely smooth.

2. The remaining 2 tablespoons of almonds, 2 tablespoons of coconut, and blueberries should be added to the smoothie before serving.

 NOTES

Calories: 360
Fat: 7g
Carbs: 16g
Protein: 9g

SPINACH & EGG SCRAMBLE WITH RASPBERRIES

INGREDIENTS

- 1 teaspoon canola oil
- 1 ½ cups baby spinach (1 1/2 ounces)
- 2 large eggs, lightly beaten
- Pinch of kosher salt
- Pinch of ground pepper
- 1 slice whole-grain bread, toasted
- ½ cup fresh raspberries

PREPARATION

1. Heat oil in a small nonstick skillet over medium-high heat.
2. Add the spinach and simmer for 1 to 2 minutes, stirring frequently, until wilted. Onto a platter, transfer the spinach. Clean the pan, then add eggs and cook it up over medium-low.
3. Cook for 1 to 2 minutes, stirring once or twice to ensure even cooking.
4. Add the spinach, salt, and pepper, and stir.
5. Along with bread and strawberries, serve the scramble.

NOTE

Calories: 296
Fat: 7g
Carbs: 21g
Protein: 10g

1 SERVING

DIFFICULT

COST

PINEAPPLE GREEN SMOOTHIE

INGREDIENTS

- ½ cup unsweetened almond milk
- ⅓ cup nonfat plain Greek yogurt
- 1 cup baby spinach
- 1 cup frozen banana slices (about 1 medium banana)
- ½ cup frozen pineapple chunks
- 1 tablespoon chia seeds
- 1-2 teaspoons pure maple syrup or honey (optional)

PREPARATION

1. Add almond milk and yogurt to a blender, then add spinach, banana, pineapple, chia seeds and sweetener (if using)
2. Blend until smooth.

NOTES

Calories: 146
Fat: 2g
Carbs: 12g
Protein: 6g

CHOCOLATE-BANANA PROTEIN SMOOTHIE

1 SERVING

DIFFICULT

COST

INGREDIENTS

- 1 banana, frozen
- ½ cup cooked red lentils
- ½ cup nonfat milk
- 2 teaspoons unsweetened cocoa powder
- 1 teaspoon pure maple syrup

PREPARATION

1. Combine banana, lentils, milk, cocoa and syrup in a blender. Puree until smooth.

NOTES

Calories: 310
Fat: 9
Carbs: 23g
Protein: 12g

1 SERVING

DIFFICULT

$ COST

RASPBERRY YOGURT CEREAL BOWL

INGREDIENTS

- 1 cup nonfat plain yogurt
- ½ cup mini shredded-wheat cereal
- ¼ cup fresh raspberries
- 2 teaspoons mini chocolate chips
- 1 teaspoon pumpkin seeds
- ¼ teaspoon ground cinnamon

PREPARATION

1. Place yogurt in a bowl and top with shredded wheat, raspberries, chocolate chips, pumpkin seeds and cinnamon.

NOTES

Calories: 290
Fat: 5g
Carbs: 22g
Protein: 12g

1 SERVING

DIFFICULT

$

COST

SPINACH & EGG TACOS

INGREDIENTS

- ¼ avocado
- 1 teaspoon lime juice
- 2 hard-boiled eggs, chopped
- 2 corn tortillas, warmed
- 1 cup chopped spinach, divided
- 2 tablespoons shredded Cheddar cheese, divided
- 2 tablespoons salsa, divided

PREPARATION

1. Smash avocado in a small bowl with lime juice and salt.
2. Mix in eggs.
3. Divide the mixture between tortillas and top each with 1/2 cup spinach and 1 tablespoon each cheese and salsa.

 NOTE.

Calories: 421
Fat: 14g
Carbs: 32g
Protein: 14g

1 SERVING

DIFFICULT

COST

REALLY GREEN SMOOTHIE

INGREDIENTS

- ¼ avocado
- 1 teaspoon lime juice
- 2 hard-boiled eggs, chopped
- 2 corn tortillas, warmed
- 1 cup chopped spinach, divided
- 2 tablespoons shredded Cheddar cheese, divided
- 2 tablespoons salsa, divided

PREPARATION

1. Smash avocado in a small bowl with lime juice and salt.
2. Mix in eggs.
3. Divide the mixture between tortillas and top each with 1/2 cup spinach and 1 tablespoon each cheese and salsa.

 NOTES

Calories: 121
Fat: 1g
Carbs: 12g
Protein: 7g

FRUIT & YOGURT SMOOTHIE

1 SERVING

DIFFICULT

COST

INGREDIENTS

- 3/4 cup nonfat plain yogurt
- 1/2 cup 100% pure fruit juice
- 1 1/2 cups (6 1/2 ounces) frozen fruit, such as blueberries, raspberries, pineapple or peaches

PREPARATION

1. Blend yogurt and juice until completely smooth. Fruit should be added through the lid's hole while the engine is running, and it should be pureed until smooth.

NOTES

Calories: 99
Fat: 2g
Carbs: 15g
Protein: 8g

BREAKFAST SALAD WITH EGG & SALSA VERDE VINAIGRETTE

INGREDIENTS

- 3 tablespoons salsa verde, such as Frontera brand
- 1 tablespoon plus 1 tsp. extra-virgin olive oil, divided
- 2 tablespoons chopped cilantro, plus more for garnish
- 2 cups mesclun or other salad greens
- 8 blue corn tortilla chips, broken into large pieces
- ½ cup canned red kidney beans, rinsed
- ¼ avocado, sliced
- 1 large egg

Calories: 167
Fat: 9g
Carbs: 22g
Protein: 11g

PREPARATION

1. In a small bowl, combine cilantro, salsa, and 1 tablespoon of oil. Place half of the mixture in a shallow dinner bowl with the mesclun (or other greens).
2. Top the salad with a layer of chips, beans, and avocado.
3. Heat the remaining 1 tsp. oil in a small nonstick skillet over medium-high heat. Add egg and cook for about two minutes, or until the white is fully cooked but the yolk is still a little runny.
4. Serve the salad with the egg. Add more cilantro, if desired, and drizzle with the leftover salsa vinaigrette.

 NOTES

MANGO-GINGER SMOOTHIE

1 SERVING

DIFFICULT

COST

INGREDIENTS

- ½ cup cooked red lentils (see Tips), cooled
- 1 cup frozen mango chunks
- ¾ cup carrot juice
- 1 teaspoon chopped fresh ginger
- 1 teaspoon honey
- Pinch of ground cardamom, plus more for garnish
- 3 ice cubes

PREPARATION

1. In a blender, combine the lentils, mango, carrot juice, ginger, honey, cardamom, and ice cubes.
2. Blend on high for 2 to 3 minutes, or until very smooth. If desired, add extra cardamom as a garnish.

Calories: 85
Fat: 1g
Carbs: 10g
Protein: 3g

 NOTE

1 SERVING

DIFFICULT

$ COST

WHITE BEAN & AVOCADO TOAST

INGREDIENTS

- 1 slice whole-wheat bread, toasted
- ¼ avocado, mashed
- ½ cup canned white beans, rinsed and drained
- Kosher salt to taste
- Ground pepper to taste
- 1 pinch Crushed red pepper

PREPARATION

1. White beans and mashed avocado go well on toast.
2. Add a sprinkle of salt, pepper, and crushed red pepper to taste.

NOTES

Calories: 120
Fat: 9g
Carbs: 21g
Protein: 9g

1 SERVING

DIFFICULT

COST

VEGAN SMOOTHIE BOWL

INGREDIENTS

- 1 large banana
- 1 cup frozen mixed berries
- ½ cup unsweetened soymilk or other unsweetened non-dairy milk
- ¼ cup pineapple chunks
- ½ kiwi, sliced
- 1 tablespoon sliced almonds, toasted if desired
- 1 tablespoon unsweetened coconut flakes, toasted if desired
- 1 teaspoon chia seeds

PREPARATION

1. In a blender, combine the banana, berries, and soymilk (or almond milk). Until smooth, blend.
2. Then, add the pineapple, kiwi, almonds, coconut, and chia seeds to the smoothie's bowl as garnish.

NOTES

Calories: 89
Fat: 5g
Carbs: 14g
Protein: 9g

1 SERVING

DIFFICULT

$ COST

PEANUT BUTTER-BANANA CINNAMON TOAST

INGREDIENTS

- 1 slice whole-wheat bread, toasted
- 1 tablespoon peanut butter
- 1 small banana, sliced
- Cinnamon to taste

PREPARATION

1. Spread toast with peanut butter and top with banana slices.
2. Sprinkle with cinnamon to taste.

NOTES

Calories: 266
Fat: 9g
Carbs: 38g
Protein: 8g

1 SERVING

DIFFICULT

COST

CANTALOUPE SMOOTHIE

INGREDIENTS

- 1 banana
- 2 cups chopped ripe cantaloupe
- 1/2 cup nonfat or low-fat plain yogurt
- 2 tablespoons nonfat dry milk
- 1 ½ tablespoons frozen orange juice concentrate
- ½ teaspoon vanilla extract

PREPARATION

1. Place unpeeled banana in the freezer overnight (or for up to 3 months).
2. Remove the banana from the freezer and let it sit until the skin begins to soften, about 2 minutes.
3. Remove the skin with a paring knife. (Don't worry if a little fiber remains.)
4. Cut the banana into chunks.
5. Add to a blender or food processor along with cantaloupe, yogurt, dry milk, orange juice and vanilla.
6. Blend until smooth.

 NOTE.

Calories: 364
Fat: 3g
Carbs: 75g
Protein: 14g

1 SERVING

DIFFICULT

$ **COST**

SPINACH-AVOCADO SMOOTHIE

INGREDIENTS

- 1 cup nonfat plain yogurt
- 1 cup fresh spinach
- 1 frozen banana
- ¼ avocado
- 2 tablespoons water
- 1 teaspoon honey

PREPARATION

1. Combine yogurt, spinach, banana, avocado, water and honey in a blender.
2. Puree until smooth.

NOTES

Calories: 257
Fat: 8g
Carbs: 28g
Protein: 16g

Meal

CHIPOTLE-LIME CAULIFLOWER TACO BOWLS

INGREDIENTS

- ¼ cup lime juice (from about 2 limes)
- 1-2 tablespoons chopped chipotles in adobo sauce (see Tip)
- 1 tablespoon honey
- 2 cloves garlic
- ½ teaspoon salt
- 1 small head cauliflower, cut into bite-size pieces
- 1 small red onion, halved and thinly sliced
- 2 cups cooked quinoa, cooled (see Associated Recipes)
- 1 cup no-salt-added canned black beans, rinsed
- ½ cup crumbled queso fresco
- 1 cup shredded red cabbage
- 1 medium avocado
- 1 lime, cut into 4 wedges (Optional)

Calories: 76
Fat: 2g
Carbs: 17g
Protein: 6g

PREPARATION

1. Set the oven to 450 degrees. Wrap foil around a sizable baking sheet with a rim.
2. Blend lime juice, honey, garlic, salt, and chipotles to taste. till largely seamless, process. In a sizable bowl, add the sauce and swirl to coat the cauliflower. To the prepared baking sheet, transfer. Toss onion on top of the cauliflower. Roast for 18 to 20 minutes, tossing once, until the cauliflower is fork-tender and browned in places. Remove from the oven and let cool.
3. Distribute the quinoa (one-half cup each) among 4 single-serving covered containers. Add two tablespoons of cheese, 1/4 cup of the black beans, and 1/4 of the cauliflower mixture to each. For up to 4 days, seal the containers and keep them chilled.
4. To reheat 1 container, vent the lid and microwave on High until steaming, 2 1/2 to 3 minutes. Top with 1/4 cup cabbage and 1/4 avocado (sliced). Serve with a lime wedge, if desired.

NOTES

VEGGIE & HUMMUS SANDWICH

1 SERVING

DIFFICULT

$ $ COST

INGREDIENTS

- 2 slices whole-grain bread
- 3 tablespoons hummus
- ¼ avocado, mashed
- ½ cup mixed salad greens
- ¼ medium red bell pepper, sliced
- ¼ cup sliced cucumber
- ¼ cup shredded carrot

PREPARATION

1. Spread hummus on one slice of bread and avocado on the other.
2. Add greens, bell pepper, cucumber, and carrot to the sandwich.
3. Cut in half, then present.

NOTE.

Calories: 125
Fat: 7g
Carbs: 20g
Protein: 13g

1 SERVING

DIFFICULT

$ COST

SPINACH & STRAWBERRY MEAL-PREP SALAD

INGREDIENTS

- 1 pound boneless, skinless chicken thighs
- ½ teaspoon kosher salt
- ½ teaspoon dried thyme
- ½ teaspoon ground pepper
- 8 cups baby spinach
- 2 cups sliced strawberries
- ¼ cup feta cheese (Optional)
- ¼ cup chopped toasted walnuts
- 6 tablespoons Balsamic Vinaigrette

Calories: 66
Fat: 3g
Carbs: 14g
Protein: 6g

PREPARATION

1. Set oven to 400 degrees Fahrenheit. Cover a baking sheet with foil or parchment paper.
2. On the prepared baking sheet, put the chicken. Add pepper, thyme, and salt liberally all over. Cook for 15 to 17 minutes, tossing the chicken once, or until the internal temperature of the chicken reaches 165°F. Slice into bite-sized pieces after setting aside to cool.
3. Divide the spinach into four 2-cup single-serving covered containers. Each dish should have one-fourth of the chicken slices, half a cup of strawberry slices, one spoonful of feta (if using), and one tablespoon of walnuts on top.
4. For up to 4 days, place the sealed salad containers in the refrigerator.
5. For up to 5 days, place 1 1/2 tablespoons of vinaigrette in each of 4 little closed containers.
6. Dress the salads with the vinaigrette just before serving.

 NOTES

SMOKED SALMON SALAD NICOISE

2 SERVINGS

DIFFICULT

COST

INGREDIENTS

- ½ small cucumber, halved, seeded and thinly sliced
- 12 small cherry or grape tomatoes, halved
- 4 ounces smoked salmon, cut into 2-inch pieces
- 8 ounces small red potatoes, scrubbed and halved
- 6 ounces green beans, preferably thin haricots verts, trimmed and halved
- 2 tablespoons reduced-fat mayonnaise
- 1 tablespoon white-wine vinegar
- 1 teaspoon lemon juice
- 1 teaspoon Worcestershire sauce
- 1 teaspoon Dijon mustard
- ½ teaspoon dried dill
- ¼ teaspoon freshly ground pepper
- 6 cups mixed salad greens

Calories: 271
Fat: 11g
Carbs: 19g
Protein: 17g

PREPARATION

1. Place a large bowl of ice water next to the stove. Bring 1 inch of water to a boil in a large saucepan.
2. Place potatoes in a steamer basket over the boiling water, cover and steam until tender when pierced with a fork, 10 to 15 minutes. Transfer the potatoes with a slotted spoon to the ice water.
3. Add green beans to the steamer, cover and steam until tender-crisp, 4 to 5 minutes. Transfer the green beans with a slotted spoon to the ice water.
4. Transfer the potatoes and beans to a towel-lined baking sheet to drain.
5. Meanwhile, whisk mayonnaise, vinegar, lemon juice, Worcestershire sauce, mustard, dill and pepper in a large bowl. Add the potatoes and green beans, salad greens, cucumber and tomatoes; toss gently to coat.
6. Divide the salad and smoked salmon between 2 plates.

NOTES

4 SERVINGS

DIFFICULT

COST

SWEET POTATO, KALE & CHICKEN SALAD WITH PEANUT DRESSING

INGREDIENTS

- 1 pound sweet potatoes (about 2 medium), scrubbed and cut into 1-inch cubes
- 1 ½ teaspoons extra-virgin olive oil
- ¼ teaspoon kosher salt
- ⅛ teaspoon ground pepper
- 1/2 cup Peanut Dressing (see Associated Recipes)
- 6 cups chopped curly kale
- 2 cups shredded cooked chicken breast (see Tip)
- ¼ cup chopped unsalted peanuts

PREPARATION

1. Set oven to 425 degrees Fahrenheit. A rimmed baking sheet should be lined with foil and lightly sprayed with cooking spray. Place aside. Sweet potatoes should be mixed with oil, salt, and pepper in a big dish.
2. Place the sweet potatoes on the baking sheet that has been prepared in a single layer. Roast for about 20 minutes, tossing once, until fork-tender and lightly browned and crispy on the exterior. Before putting together bowls, set aside to chill.
3. Put two tablespoons of peanut dressing into each of four tiny containers with lids, and then store in the fridge for up to four days.
4. ·Divide the kale (approximately 1 1/2 cups total) among the 4 single-serving containers. Top each with 1/4 of the sweet potatoes that have been cooked and 1/2 cup of the chicken. For up to 4 days, seal the containers and keep them chilled.
5. Just before serving, drizzle each salad with 1 portion of peanut dressing and toss well to coat. Top with 1 tablespoon chopped peanuts

NOTES

Calories: 293
Fat: 9g
Carbs: 32g
Protein: 12g

MEAL-PREP VEGAN LETTUCE WRAPS

4 SERVINGS

DIFFICULT

COST

INGREDIENTS

- 2 heads butter or Bibb lettuce, leaves separated
- 1 1/2 cups cooked quinoa, cooled to room temperature (see Associated Recipes)
- 4 cups Bean Salad with Lemon-Cumin Dressing (see Associated Recipes)
- ⅓ cup chopped fresh mint (reserved from bean salad recipe)

PREPARATION

1. To prepare 1 serving of lettuce wraps: Place 3 lettuce leaves in a single-serving lidded container. Top each leaf with 2 tablespoons quinoa and 1/3 cup bean salad.
2. Sprinkle each with 1 1/2 teaspoons mint. Refrigerate for up to 1 day.

 NOTE.

Calories: 425
Fat: 20g
Carbs: 50g
Protein: 14g

4 SERVINGS

DIFFICULT

$ **COST**

MASON JAR POWER SALAD WITH CHICKPEAS & TUNA

INGREDIENTS

- 3 cups bite-sized pieces chopped kale
- 2 tablespoons honey-mustard vinaigrette (see associated recipe)
- 1 2.5-ounce pouch tuna in water
- ½ cup rinsed canned chickpeas
- 1 carrot, peeled and shredded

PREPARATION

1. Toss kale and dressing in a bowl, then tranfer to a 1-quart mason jar.
2. Top with tuna, chickpeas and carrot. Screw lid onto the jar and refrigerate for up to 2 days.
3. To serve, empty the jar contents into a bowl and toss to combine the salad ingredients with the dressed kale.

NOTES

Calories: 430
Fat: 23g
Carbs: 30g
Protein: 26g

WINTER KALE & QUINOA SALAD WITH AVOCADO

INGREDIENTS

- 1 small sweet potato, peeled and cut into 1/2-inch pieces (1 1/2 cups)
- 2 ½ teaspoons olive oil, divided
- ½ avocado
- 1 tablespoon lime juice
- 1 clove garlic, peeled
- ½ teaspoon ground cumin
- ⅛ teaspoon salt
- ⅛ teaspoon ground pepper
- 1-2 tablespoons water
- 1 cup cooked quinoa (see Associated Recipes)
- ¾ cup no-salt-added canned black beans, rinsed
- 1 ½ cups chopped baby kale
- 2 tablespoons pepitas (see Tip)
- 1 scallion, chopped

Calories: 189
Fat: 10g
Carbs: 24g
Protein: 15g

PREPARATION

1. Set oven to 400 degrees Fahrenheit.
2. On a sizable rimmed baking sheet, toss sweet potatoes with 1 teaspoon oil. Roast for about 25 minutes, stirring once halfway through, until fork-tender.
3. In the meantime, blend or process the remaining 1 1/2 teaspoons of oil, avocado, lime juice, garlic, cumin, salt, and pepper along with 1 tablespoon of water until smooth. If necessary, add 1 Tbsp. water to achieve the appropriate consistency.
4. In a medium bowl, mix the kale, black beans, sweet potatoes, and quinoa. Add the avocado dressing and toss to evenly coat. Add pepitas and scallion on top.

NOTES

VEGAN SUPERFOOD GRAIN BOWLS

4 SERVINGS

DIFFICULT

$ COST

INGREDIENTS

- 1 (8 ounce) pouch microwavable quinoa
- ½ cup hummus
- 2 tablespoons lemon juice
- 1 (5 ounce) package baby kale
- 1 (8 ounce) package refrigerated cooked whole baby beets, sliced (or 2 cups from salad bar)
- 1 cup frozen shelled edamame, thawed
- 1 medium avocado, sliced
- ¼ cup unsalted toasted sunflower seeds

Calories: 139
Fat: 4g
Carbs: 24g
Protein: 5g

PREPARATION

1. Prepare quinoa according to package directions; set aside to cool.
2. Combine hummus and lemon juice in a small bowl. Thin with water to desired dressing consistency. Divide the dressing among 4 small condiment containers with lids and refrigerate.
3. Divide baby kale among 4 single-serving containers with lids. Top each with 1/2 cup of the quinoa, 1/2 cup beets, 1/4 cup edamame and 1 tablespoon sunflower seeds.
4. When ready to eat, top with 1/4 avocado and the hummus dressing.

NOTES

SLOW-COOKER CHICKEN & CHICKPEA SOUP

6 SERVINGS

DIFFICULT

COST

INGREDIENTS

- 1 ½ cups dried chickpeas, soaked overnight
- 4 cups water
- 1 large yellow onion, finely chopped
- 1 (15 ounce) can no-salt-added diced tomatoes, preferably fire-roasted
- 2 tablespoons tomato paste
- 4 cloves garlic, finely chopped
- 1 bay leaf
- 4 teaspoons ground cumin
- 4 teaspoons paprika
- ¼ teaspoon cayenne pepper
- ¼ teaspoon ground pepper
- 2 pounds bone-in chicken thighs, skin removed, trimmed
- 1 (14 ounce) can artichoke hearts, drained and quartered
- ¼ cup halved pitted oil-cured olives
- ½ teaspoon salt
- ¼ cup chopped fresh parsley or cilantro

PREPARATION

1. Chickpeas should be drained and added to a 6-quart or larger slow cooker. Stir together the water, onion, tomatoes, tomato juice, tomato paste, bay leaf, cumin, paprika, cayenne, and pepper.Add, Cook, and cover for 8 hours on low or 4 hours on high.
2. Place the chicken on a spotless cutting board, then allow it to cool slightly. Remove the bay leaf. add the artichokes, olives, and salt in the slow cooker.
3. Discard the chicken's bones as you shred it. Add the chicken to the soup and stir. Serve garnished with cilantro or parsley.

 NOTE.

Calories: 77
Fats: 4g
Crabs: 17g
Protein: 6g

ROASTED ROOT VEGETABLES WITH GOAT CHEESE POLENTA

INGREDIENTS

- Polenta:
- 2 cups low-sodium vegetable or chicken broth
- ½ cup polenta fine cornmeal or corn grits
- ¼ cup goat cheese
- 1 tablespoon extra-virgin olive oil or butter
- ¼ teaspoon kosher salt
- ¼ teaspoon ground pepper
- Vegetables:
- 1 tablespoon extra-virgin olive oil or butter
- 1 clove garlic, smashed
- 2 cups roasted root vegetables (see associated recipes)
- 1 tablespoon torn fresh sage
- 2 teaspoons prepared pesto
- Fresh parsley for garnish

PREPARATION

1. To prepare polenta: Bring broth to a boil in a medium saucepan. Reduce heat to low and gradually add polenta (or cornmeal or grits), whisking vigorously to avoid clumping. Cover and cook for 10 minutes. Stir, cover and continue cooking until thickened and creamy, about 10 minutes more. Stir in goat cheese, oil (or butter), salt and pepper.
2. To prepare vegetables: Heat oil (or butter) in a medium skillet over medium heat. Add garlic and cook, stirring, until fragrant, about 1 minute. Add roasted vegetables and cook, stirring often, until heated through, 2 to 4 minutes. Stir in sage and cook until fragrant, about 1 minute more.
3. Serve the vegetables over the polenta, topped with pesto. Garnish with parsley, if desired.

 **NOTES**

Calories: 162
Fat: 8g
Carbs: 21g
Protein: 9g

EGGPLANT PARMESAN

6 SERVINGS

DIFFICULT

$ $ COST

INGREDIENTS

- Canola or olive oil cooking spray
- 2 large eggs
- 2 tablespoons water
- 1 cup panko breadcrumbs
- ¾ cup grated Parmesan cheese, divided
- 1 teaspoon Italian seasoning
- 2 medium eggplants (about 2 pounds total), cut crosswise into ¼-inch-thick slices
- ½ teaspoon salt
- ½ teaspoon ground pepper
- 1 (24 ounce) jar no-salt-added tomato sauce
- ¼ cup fresh basil leaves, torn, plus more for serving
- 2 cloves garlic, grated
- ½ teaspoon crushed red pepper
- 1 cup shredded part-skim mozzarella cheese, divided

Calories: 241
Fat: 9g
Carbs: 28g
Protein: 14g

PREPARATION

1. ·Position racks in middle and lower thirds of oven; preheat to 400°F. Coat 2 baking sheets and a 9-by-13-inch baking dish with cooking spray.
2. ·Whisk eggs and water in a shallow bowl. Mix breadcrumbs, 1/4 cup Parmesan and Italian seasoning in another shallow dish. Dip eggplant in the egg mixture, then coat with the breadcrumb mixture, gently pressing to adhere.
3. ·Arrange the eggplant in a single layer on the prepared baking sheets. Generously spray both sides of the eggplant with cooking spray. Bake, flipping the eggplant and switching the pans between racks halfway, until the eggplant is tender and lightly browned, about 30 minutes. Season with salt and pepper.
4. ·Meanwhile, mix tomato sauce, basil, garlic and crushed red pepper in a medium bowl.
5. ·Spread about 1/2 cup of the sauce in the prepared baking dish. Arrange half the eggplant slices over the sauce. Spoon 1 cup sauce over the eggplant and sprinkle with 1/4 cup Parmesan and 1/2 cup mozzarella. Top with the remaining eggplant, sauce and cheese.
6. ·Bake until the sauce is bubbling and the top is golden, 20 to 30 minutes. Let cool for 5 minutes. Sprinkle with more basil before serving, if desired.

4 SERVINGS

DIFFICULT

$ COST

CHICKEN-QUINOA BOWL WITH OLIVES & CUCUMBER

INGREDIENTS

- 1 pound boneless, skinless chicken breasts, trimmed
- ¼ teaspoon salt
- ¼ teaspoon ground pepper
- 1 7-ounce jar roasted red peppers, rinsed
- ¼ cup slivered almonds
- 4 tablespoons extra-virgin olive oil, divided
- 1 small clove garlic, crushed
- 1 teaspoon paprika
- ½ teaspoon ground cumin
- ¼ teaspoon crushed red pepper (Optional)
- 2 cups cooked quinoa
- ¼ cup pitted Kalamata olives, chopped
- ¼ cup finely chopped red onion
- 1 cup diced cucumber
- ¼ cup crumbled feta cheese
- 2 tablespoons finely chopped fresh parsley

Calories: 291
Fat: 7g
Carbs: 21g
Protein: 14g

PREPARATION

1. Place a rack in the upper third of the oven and turn the broiler to high. Use foil to cover a baking sheet with a rim.
2. Place the chicken on the prepared baking sheet, seasoning with salt and pepper. For 14 to 18 minutes, broil, stirring once, until an instant-read thermometer inserted in the thickest section registers 165 degrees F. Slice or shred the chicken after moving it to a clean cutting board.
3. In the meantime, combine the peppers, almonds, 2 tablespoons of oil, the garlic, paprika, cumin, and any crushed red pepper you're using in a small food processor. until largely smooth, puree.
4. In a medium bowl, mix the quinoa, olives, red onion, and the last 2 tablespoons of oil.
5. Divide the quinoa mixture among four bowls to serve, then top each with equal quantities of cucumber, chicken, and the red pepper sauce. Sprinkle with feta and parsley.

 **NOTES**

_____
_____
_____
_____

4 SERVINGS

DIFFICULT

$ $ COST

WALNUT-ROSEMARY CRUSTED SALMON

INGREDIENTS

- 2 teaspoons Dijon mustard
- 1 clove garlic, minced
- ¼ teaspoon lemon zest
- 1 teaspoon lemon juice
- 1 teaspoon chopped fresh rosemary
- ½ teaspoon honey
- ½ teaspoon kosher salt
- ¼ teaspoon crushed red pepper
- 3 tablespoons panko breadcrumbs
- 3 tablespoons finely chopped walnuts
- 1 teaspoon extra-virgin olive oil
- 1 (1 pound) skinless salmon fillet, fresh or frozen
- Olive oil cooking spray
- Chopped fresh parsley and lemon wedges for garnish

PREPARATION

1. Set oven to 425 degrees Fahrenheit. Use parchment paper to line a big baking sheet with a rim.
2. In a small bowl, mix the mustard, garlic, lemon zest, lemon juice, rosemary, honey, salt, and red pepper flakes. In a different small bowl, mix the panko, walnuts, and oil.
3. On the prepared baking sheet, put the fish. After applying the mustard mixture to the fish, sprinkle the panko mixture over it and press firmly to help it stick. Apply cooking spray sparingly.
4. Depending on thickness, bake the fish for 8 to 12 minutes, or until it flakes easily with a fork.
5. If preferred, serve with lemon wedges and garnish with parsley.

 **NOTE.**

Calories: 222
Fat: 12g
Carbs: 21g
Protein: 14g

HASSELBACK EGGPLANT PARMESAN

4 SERVINGS

DIFFICULT

COST

INGREDIENTS

- 1 cup prepared low-sodium marinara sauce
- 4 small eggplants (about 6 inches long; 1 3/4 pounds total)
- 2 tablespoons extra-virgin olive oil plus 2 teaspoons, divided
- 4 ounces fresh mozzarella, thinly sliced into 12 pieces
- ¼ cup prepared pesto
- ½ cup whole-wheat panko breadcrumbs
- 2 tablespoons grated Parmesan cheese
- 1 tablespoon chopped fresh basil

Calories: 349
Fat: 11g
Carbs: 24g
Protein: 11g

PREPARATION

1. Set oven to 375 degrees Fahrenheit.
2. In a 9 by 13-inch baking dish that may be used for broiling, spread sauce. Slice each eggplant crosswise every 1/4 inch, almost to the bottom but not all the way through. Transfer the eggplants with care to the baking pan. To make the cuts more visible, gently fan them. Sprinkle the eggplants with 2 tablespoons of oil. Alternately place mozzarella and pesto inside the cuts; some cuts might not be filled. Wrap with foil.
3. Bake the eggplants for 45 to 55 minutes, or until very soft.
4. In a separate dish, mix the remaining 2 teaspoons oil, panko, and Parmesan. Take off the foil and sprinkle the breadcrumb mixture over the eggplants.
5. Increase the oven temperature to broil. The topping should be golden brown after 2 to 4 minutes of broiling the eggplants on the center rack. Add basil on top. With the sauce, serve.

 NOTES

69

CHICKEN & VEGETABLE PENNE WITH PARSLEY-WALNUT PESTO

4 SERVINGS

DIFFICULT

COST

INGREDIENTS

- ¾ cup chopped walnuts
- 1 cup lightly packed parsley leaves
- 2 cloves garlic, crushed and peeled
- ½ teaspoon plus 1/8 teaspoon salt
- ⅛ teaspoon ground pepper
- 2 tablespoons olive oil
- ⅓ cup grated Parmesan cheese
- 1 ½ cups shredded or sliced cooked skinless chicken breast (8 oz.)
- 6 ounces whole-wheat penne or fusilli pasta (1 3/4 cups)
- 8 ounces green beans, trimmed and halved crosswise (2 cups)
- 2 cups cauliflower florets (8 oz.)

Calories: 414
Fat: 7g
Carbs: 23g
Protein: 18g

PREPARATION

1. Bring water in a big pot to a boil.
2. In a small bowl, add the walnuts. Microwave on High for 2 to 2 1/2 minutes, or until fragrant and lightly toasted. (Alternatively, toast the walnuts for 2 to 3 minutes, stirring regularly, in a small, dry skillet over medium-low heat.) Place on a plate and allow to cool. Set aside 1/4 cup for the topping.
3. In a food processor, mix the remaining 1/2 cup of walnuts, parsley, garlic, salt, and pepper. Process the nuts until they are powdered. Oil should be added gradually through the feed tube while the motor is operating. Then pulse to incorporate the Parmesan. Put the pesto in a big bowl by scraping it. Add chicken.
4. During this time, cook the pasta for 4 minutes in the boiling water. Add the cauliflower and green beans; cover the pan and cook for an additional 5 to 7 minutes, or until the veggies are soft and the pasta is almost done. Scoop off 3/4 cup of the cooking liquid before draining, then swirl it into the pesto-chicken combination to slightly warm it.
5. Add the pasta and vegetables after draining them to the chicken and pesto mixture. Toss to evenly coat.
6. Top each meal with one tablespoon of the saved walnuts after dividing among the four spaghetti bowls.

4 SERVINGS

DIFFICULT

COST

SHEET-PAN CHICKEN WITH ROASTED SPRING VEGETABLES & LEMON

INGREDIENTS

- Lemon Vinaigrette
- 1 lemon
- 1 tablespoon olive oil
- 1 tablespoon crumbled feta cheese
- ½ teaspoon honey
- Greek Chicken with Roasted Spring Vegetables
- 2 (8 ounce) skinless, boneless chicken breast halves, cut in half lengthwise
- ¼ cup light mayonnaise
- 6 cloves garlic, minced
- ½ cup panko bread crumbs
- 3 tablespoons grated Parmesan cheese
- ½ teaspoon kosher salt
- ½ teaspoon black pepper
- Nonstick olive oil cooking spray
- 2 cups 1-inch pieces asparagus
- 1 ½ cups sliced fresh cremini mushrooms
- 1 ½ cups halved grape tomatoes
- 1 tablespoon olive oil
- Snipped fresh dill

PREPARATION

1. Prepare vinaigrette: Remove 1/2 teaspoon zest and squeeze 1 tablespoon juice from lemon. In a small bowl whisk together lemon zest and juice and the remaining ingredients. Set aside.

2. Prepare chicken and vegetables: Place a 15x10-inch baking pan in oven. Preheat oven to 475 degrees F.

3. Meanwhile, using the flat side of a meat mallet, flatten chicken between two pieces of plastic wrap until 1/2 inch thick.

4. Place chicken in a medium bowl. Add mayonnaise and 2 of the garlic cloves; stir to coat. In a shallow dish stir together bread crumbs, cheese, 1/4 teaspoon of the salt, and 1/4 teaspoon of the pepper. Dip chicken into crumb mixture, turning to coat. Lightly coat tops of chicken with cooking spray.

5. In a large bowl combine asparagus, mushrooms, tomatoes, oil and the remaining 4 cloves garlic and 1/4 teaspoon salt and pepper.

6. Carefully place chicken in one end of hot pan and place asparagus mixture in other end of pan. Roast 18 to 20 minutes or until chicken is done (165 degrees F) and vegetables are tender.

7. Drizzle chicken and vegetables with vinaigrette and sprinkle with dill.

CHICKEN CAESAR PASTA SALAD

6 SERVINGS

DIFFICULT

$ COST

INGREDIENTS

- ½ cup low-fat buttermilk
- ¼ cup low-fat plain Greek yogurt
- 3 tablespoons extra-virgin olive oil
- 2 tablespoons fresh lemon juice
- 2 teaspoons Dijon mustard
- 1 ½ teaspoons anchovy paste
- 1 large garlic clove
- ¾ cup finely grated Parmesan cheese, divided
- ½ teaspoon salt, divided
- ½ teaspoon ground pepper, divided
- 8 ounces whole-wheat penne
- 3 cups shredded cooked chicken breast
- 1 pint cherry tomatoes, halved
- 5 cups chopped romaine lettuce

Calories: 383
Fat: 10g
Carbs: 24g
Protein: 13g

PREPARATION

1. Blend the buttermilk, yogurt, oil, lemon juice, mustard, anchovy paste, garlic, 1/2 cup Parmesan, 1/4 teaspoon salt, and 1/4 teaspoon pepper in a high-speed blender for about a minute, or until creamy. Place aside.
2. Without adding salt, prepare pasta as directed on the package. Reserving 1 cup of cooking water, drain.
3. In a sizable bowl, combine the pasta, chicken, tomatoes, 1/4 cup of the cooking water that was set aside, and the final 1/4 teaspoons of salt and pepper. Add the buttermilk dressing and stir until well mixed. If more cooking water is required to achieve a creamy consistency, stir it in. For at least 30 minutes or up to two days, cover and chill.
4. Add lettuce and the remaining 1/4 cup Parmesan right before serving.

 NOTE

4 SERVINGS

DIFFICULT

COST

DIJON SALMON WITH GREEN BEAN PILAF

INGREDIENTS

- 1 ¼ pounds wild salmon (see Tip), skinned and cut into 4 portions
- 3 tablespoons extra-virgin olive oil, divided
- 1 tablespoon minced garlic
- ¾ teaspoon salt
- 2 tablespoons mayonnaise
- 2 teaspoons whole-grain mustard
- ½ teaspoon ground pepper, divided
- 12 ounces pretrimmed haricots verts or thin green beans, cut into thirds
- 1 small lemon, zested and cut into 4 wedges
- 2 tablespoons pine nuts
- 1 8-ounce package precooked brown rice
- 2 tablespoons water
- Chopped fresh parsley for garnish

PREPARATION

1. Preheat oven to 425 degrees F. Line a rimmed baking sheet with foil or parchment paper.
2. Brush salmon with 1 tablespoon oil and place on the prepared baking sheet. Mash garlic and salt into a paste with the side of a chef's knife or a fork. Combine a scant 1 teaspoon of the garlic paste in a small bowl with mayonnaise, mustard and 1/4 teaspoon pepper. Spread the mixture on top of the fish.
3. Roast the salmon until it flakes easily with a fork in the thickest part, 6 to 8 minutes per inch of thickness.
4. Meanwhile, heat the remaining 2 tablespoons oil in a large skillet over medium-high heat. Add green beans, lemon zest, pine nuts, the remaining garlic paste and 1/4 teaspoon pepper; cook, stirring, until the beans are just tender, 2 to 4 minutes. Reduce heat to medium. Add rice and water and cook, stirring, until hot, 2 to 3 minutes more.
5. Sprinkle the salmon with parsley, if desired, and serve with the green bean pilaf and lemon wedges.

 **NOTES**

Calories: 442
Fat: 25g
Carbs: 12g
Protein: 32g

SLOW-COOKER VEGETARIAN BOLOGNESE

DIFFICULT

COST

INGREDIENTS

- 1 (28 ounce) can diced tomatoes, preferably San Marzano
- ½ cup dry white wine
- ½ cup low-sodium vegetable broth or water
- 1 cup chopped onion
- ½ cup chopped celery
- ½ cup chopped carrot
- 3 tablespoons extra-virgin olive oil
- 2 tablespoons minced garlic
- 1 teaspoon Italian seasoning
- ½ teaspoon salt
- ¼ teaspoon ground pepper
- 2 (15 ounce) cans no-salt-added cannellini beans or small white beans, rinsed
- ¼ cup heavy cream
- 1 pound whole-wheat pasta
- ½ cup grated Parmesan cheese
- ¼ cup chopped fresh basil

PREPARATION

1. In a 5- to 6-quart slow cooker, combine the tomatoes, wine, broth (or water), onion, celery, carrot, oil, garlic, Italian seasoning, salt, and pepper.
2. Cook for 4 hours on high or 8 hours on low. At the end of the cooking process, stir in the beans and cream. Stay warm.
3. In the meantime, heat up a sizable pot of water to a boil. Drain spaghetti after cooking it according the directions on the package. 8 bowls should get the pasta. Add basil, Parmesan, and sauce as a garnish.

 NOTES

Calories: 434
Fat: 13g
Carbs: 34g
Protein: 11g

CREAMY LEMON PASTA WITH SHRIMP

4 SERVINGS

DIFFICULT

$ $

COST

INGREDIENTS

- 8 ounces whole-wheat fettuccine
- 1 tablespoon extra-virgin olive oil
- 12 ounces peeled and deveined raw shrimp (21-25 count)
- 2 tablespoons unsalted butter
- 1 tablespoon finely chopped garlic
- ¼ teaspoon crushed red pepper
- 4 cups loosely packed arugula
- ¼ cup whole-milk plain yogurt
- 1 teaspoon lemon zest
- 2 tablespoons lemon juice
- ¼ teaspoon salt
- ⅓ cup grated Parmesan cheese, plus more for garnish
- ¼ cup thinly sliced fresh basil

Calories: 403
Fat: 14g
Carbs: 36g
Protein: 18g

PREPARATION

1. 7 cups of water should come to a boil. Stir the fettuccine to separate the noodles before adding. Cook for 7 to 9 minutes, or until the meat is barely tender. After draining, save 1/2 cup of the cooking liquid.
2. Over medium-high heat, warm oil in a sizable nonstick skillet. Add the shrimp and cook, stirring periodically, for 2 to 3 minutes, or until pink and curled. Put the shrimp in a basin.
3. Reduce heat to medium, then add butter to the pan. Stir often while cooking the garlic and crushed red pepper for approximately a minute, or until the garlic is aromatic. Arugula should be added and cooked for about a minute while stirring. Low-heat setting. When the pasta is thoroughly coated and creamy, add the remaining 1/4 cup of cooking water, the yogurt, the lemon zest, and the fettuccine.
4. Add the salt, lemon juice, and shrimp while tossing the fettuccine to coat. Take the dish off the heat, then top with Parmesan.
5. If preferred, top the fettuccine with additional Parmesan and basil.

4 SERVINGS

DIFFICULT

$ $

COST

ROASTED SALMON WITH SMOKY CHICKPEAS & GREENS

INGREDIENTS

- 2 tablespoons extra-virgin olive oil, divided
- 1 tablespoon smoked paprika
- ½ teaspoon salt, divided, plus a pinch
- 1 (15 ounce) can no-salt-added chickpeas, rinsed
- ⅓ cup buttermilk
- ¼ cup mayonnaise
- ¼ cup chopped fresh chives and/or dill, plus more for garnish
- ½ teaspoon ground pepper, divided
- ¼ teaspoon garlic powder
- 10 cups chopped kale
- ¼ cup water
- 1 ¼ pounds wild salmon, cut into 4 portions
- ¼ avocado

Calories: 447
Fat: 22g
Carbs: 23g
Protein: 37g

PREPARATION

1. Position racks in upper third and middle of oven; preheat to 425 degrees F.
2. Combine 1 tablespoon oil, paprika and 1/4 teaspoon salt in a medium bowl. Very thoroughly pat chickpeas dry, then toss with the paprika mixture. Spread on a rimmed baking sheet. Bake the chickpeas on the upper rack, stirring twice, for 30 minutes.
3. Meanwhile, puree buttermilk, mayonnaise, herbs, 1/4 teaspoon pepper and garlic powder in a blender until smooth. Set aside.
4. Heat the remaining 1 tablespoon oil in a large skillet over medium heat. Add kale and cook, stirring occasionally, for 2 minutes.
5. Add water and continue cooking until the kale is tender, about 5 minutes more. Remove from heat and stir in a pinch of salt.
6. Remove the chickpeas from the oven and push them to one side of the pan. Place salmon on the other side and season with the remaining 1/4 teaspoon each salt and pepper. Bake until the salmon is just cooked through, 5 to 8 minutes.
7. Drizzle the reserved dressing on the salmon, garnish with more herbs and avocado, if desired, and serve with the kale and chickpeas.

SLOW-COOKER VEGETARIAN BOLOGNESE

6 SERVINGS

DIFFICULT

$ $ COST

INGREDIENTS

- 2 cups chopped onions
- 1 cup chopped carrots
- 1 cup chopped celery
- 1 pound cooked Meal-Prep Sheet-Pan Chicken Thighs (see associated recipe), diced
- 4 cups cooked whole-wheat rotini pasta
- 6 cups reduced-sodium chicken broth
- 4 teaspoons dried Italian seasoning
- ¼ teaspoon salt
- 1 (15 ounce) can no-salt-added white beans, rinsed
- 4 cups baby spinach (half of a 5-ounce box)
- 4 tablespoons chopped fresh basil, divided (Optional)
- 2 tablespoons best-quality extra-virgin olive oil
- ½ cup grated Parmigiano-Reggiano cheese

PREPARATION

1. Put celery, carrots, and onions in a sizable plastic bag that can be sealed. Place cooked pasta and cold chicken in a separate bag. Freeze for up to five days after sealing both bags. Before continuing, let the bags defrost overnight in the fridge.

2. Transfer the vegetable mixture to a large slow cooker. Add broth, Italian seasoning, and salt. Cover and cook on Low for 7 1/4 hours.

3. Add the defrosted chicken, pasta, beans, spinach, and any additional 2 tablespoons of basil.

4. Cook for a further 45 minutes. Put the soup in bowls by ladling. Add a few drops of oil to each bowl before adding cheese and, if wanted, the final 2 tablespoons of basil.

NOTES

Calories: 457
Fat: 14g
Carbs: 32g
Protein: 14g

4 SERVINGS

DIFFICULT

$ $

COST

SALMON COUSCOUS SALAD

INGREDIENTS

- ¼ cup sliced cremini mushrooms
- ¼ cup diced eggplant
- 3 cups baby spinach
- 2 tablespoons white-wine vinaigrette, divided (see Tip)
- ¼ cup cooked Israeli couscous, preferably whole-wheat
- 4 ounces cooked salmon
- ¼ cup sliced dried apricots
- 2 tablespoons crumbled goat cheese (1/2 ounce)

PREPARATION

1. Apply cooking spray to a small skillet and heat it over medium-high heat. Add the mushrooms and eggplant; simmer, stirring occasionally, for 3 to 5 minutes, or until the juices have released. Heat has been removed; set aside.
2. Put spinach on a 9-inch platter and toss with 1 Tbsp plus 1 tsp of vinaigrette.
3. Place the couscous on top of the spinach and toss with the remaining 2 teaspoons of vinaigrette. Afterward, add the salmon.
4. Add goat cheese, dried apricots, and cooked vegetables on top.

 NOTES

Calories: 464
Fat: 22g
Carbs: 35g
Protein: 25g

QUINOA POWER SALAD

2 SERVINGS

DIFFICULT

$ COST

INGREDIENTS

- 1 medium sweet potato, peeled and cut into 1/2-inch-thick wedges
- ½ red onion, cut into 1/4-inch-thick wedges
- 2 tablespoons extra-virgin olive oil, divided
- ½ teaspoon garlic powder
- ¼ teaspoon salt, divided
- 8 ounces chicken tenders
- 2 tablespoons whole-grain mustard, divided
- 1 tablespoon finely chopped shallot
- 1 tablespoon pure maple syrup
- 1 tablespoon cider vinegar
- 4 cups baby greens, such as spinach, kale and/or arugula, washed and dried
- ½ cup cooked red quinoa, cooled
- 1 tablespoon unsalted sunflower seeds, toasted
- 3 tomatoes

Calories: 266
Fat: 5g
Carbs: 25g
Protein: 11g

PREPARATION

1. Set oven to 425 degrees Fahrenheit. In a larger bowl, combine sweet potato and onion with 1 tablespoon oil, 1/8 teaspoon salt, and garlic powder. Spread out and roast for 15 minutes on a big baking sheet with a rim.
2. In the meantime, add the chicken to the bowl and stir in 1 tablespoon of mustard. Remove the vegetables from the oven after 15 minutes of roasting and toss. To the pan, add the chicken. Return to the oven and roast for an additional 10 minutes or until the chicken is fully cooked and the vegetables are starting to brown. Take out of the oven, then allow to cool.
3. In the meantime, combine the shallot, vinegar, maple syrup, 1 tablespoon of residual oil, 1 tablespoon of mustard, and 1/8 teaspoon of salt in the big bowl.
4. Once the chicken has cooled, shred it and add it to the dressing in a bowl. Add the roasted vegetables, sliced tomatoes, quinoa, and baby greens. Add the sunflower seeds and toss with the dressing.

SLOW-COOKER CHICKEN & ORZO WITH TOMATOES & OLIVES

INGREDIENTS

- 1 pound boneless, skinless chicken breasts, trimmed
- 1 cup low-sodium chicken broth
- 2 medium tomatoes, chopped
- 1 medium onion, halved and sliced
- Zest and juice of 1 lemon
- 1 teaspoon herbes de Provence
- ½ teaspoon salt
- ½ teaspoon ground pepper
- ¾ cup whole-wheat orzo
- ⅓ cup quartered black or green olives
- 2 tablespoons chopped fresh parsley

Calories: 278
Fat: 5g
Carbs: 30g
Protein: 29g

PREPARATION

1. Cut each half of a chicken breast into four pieces. In a 6-quart slow cooker, mix the chicken, broth, tomatoes, onion, lemon zest, lemon juice, herbes de Provence, salt, and pepper.
2. Cook for 1 hour and 30 minutes on high or 3 hours and 30 minutes on low.
3. Add the orzo and olives, cover, and simmer for an additional 30 minutes or until the orzo is cooked. Allow to cool a bit.
4. Parsley should be added just before serving.

NOTE.

4 SERVINGS

DIFFICULT

$ COST

SALMON & ASPARAGUS WITH LEMON-GARLIC BUTTER SAUCE

INGREDIENTS

- 1 pound center-cut salmon fillet, preferably wild, cut into 4 portions
- 1 pound fresh asparagus, trimmed
- ½ teaspoon salt
- ½ teaspoon ground pepper
- 3 tablespoons butter
- 1 tablespoon extra-virgin olive oil
- ½ tablespoon grated garlic
- 1 teaspoon grated lemon zest
- 1 tablespoon lemon juice

Calories: 270
Fat: 15g
Carbs: 12g
Protein: 20g

PREPARATION

1. Set oven to 375 degrees Fahrenheit. Spray cooking oil on a sizable baking sheet with a rim.
2. Place the asparagus and salmon on opposite sides of the baking sheet that has been prepared. Add salt and pepper to the fish and asparagus.
3. In a small skillet over medium heat, combine the butter, oil, garlic, lemon juice, and zest. Cook until the butter is melted. Over the salmon and asparagus, drizzle the butter mixture.
4. Bake for 12 to 15 minutes, or until the salmon is thoroughly cooked and the asparagus is barely tender.

4 SERVINGS

DIFFICULT

$ COST

ONE-POT GARLICKY SHRIMP & SPINACH

INGREDIENTS

- 3 tablespoons extra-virgin olive oil, divided
- 6 medium cloves garlic, sliced, divided
- 1 pound spinach
- ¼ teaspoon salt plus 1/8 teaspoon, divided
- 1 ½ teaspoons lemon zest
- 1 tablespoon lemon juice
- 1 pound shrimp (21-30 count), peeled and deveined
- ¼ teaspoon crushed red pepper
- 1 tablespoon finely chopped fresh parsl

Calories: 226
Fat: 12g
Carbs: 6g
Protein: 26g

PREPARATION

1. Heat 1 tablespoon oil in a large pot over medium heat. Add half the garlic and cook until beginning to brown, 1 to 2 minutes. Add spinach and 1/4 teaspoon salt and toss to coat. Cook, stirring once or twice, until mostly wilted, 3 to 5 minutes. Remove from heat and stir in lemon juice. Transfer to a bowl and keep warm.
2. Increase heat to medium-high and add the remaining 2 tablespoons oil to the pot. Add the remaining garlic and cook until beginning to brown, 1 to 2 minutes.
3. Add shrimp, crushed red pepper and the remaining 1/8 teaspoon salt; cook, stirring, until the shrimp are just cooked through, 3 to 5 minutes more.
4. Serve the shrimp over the spinach, sprinkled with lemon zest and parsley.

 **NOTES**

FIG & GOAT CHEESE SALAD

1 SERVING

DIFFICULT

$ COST

INGREDIENTS

- 2 cups mixed salad greens
- 4 dried figs, stemmed and sliced
- 1 ounce fresh goat cheese, crumbled
- 1 ½ tablespoons slivered almonds, preferably toasted
- 2 teaspoons extra-virgin olive oil
- 2 teaspoons balsamic vinegar
- ½ teaspoon honey
- Pinch of salt
- Freshly ground pepper to taste

PREPARATION

1. ·Combine greens, figs, goat cheese and almonds in a medium bowl. Stir together oil, vinegar, honey, salt and pepper.
2. ·Just before serving, drizzle the dressing over the salad and toss.

 NOTES

Calories: 140
Fat: 9g
Carbs: 32g
Protein: 10g

CHICKEN PESTO PASTA WITH ASPARAGUS

6 SERVINGS

DIFFICULT

$ COST

INGREDIENTS

- 8 ounces whole-wheat penne
- 1 pound fresh asparagus, trimmed and cut into 2-inch pieces
- 3 cups shredded cooked chicken breast
- 1 (7 ounce) container refrigerated basil pesto
- 1 teaspoon salt
- ¼ teaspoon ground pepper
- 1 ounce Parmesan cheese, grated (about 1/4 cup)
- Small fresh basil leaves for garnish

Calories: 422
Fat: 9g
Carbs: 25g
Protein: 14g

PREPARATION

1. According to the directions on the package, cook the pasta in a big saucepan. Asparagus should be added to the pot during the last two minutes of cooking. Reserving 1/2 cup of cooking water, drain.
2. Add the chicken, pesto, salt, and pepper to the spaghetti mixture before adding it back to the saucepan. To get the appropriate consistency, stir in the reserved cooking water, 1 tablespoon at a time.
3. Transfer the mixture to a serving dish, top with Parmesan, and, if preferred, add basil. Serve right away.

NOTE

EASY SALMON CAKES

4 SERVINGS

DIFFICULT

COST

INGREDIENTS

- 3 teaspoons extra-virgin olive oil, divided
- 1 small onion, finely chopped
- 1 stalk celery, finely diced
- 2 tablespoons chopped fresh parsley
- 15 ounces canned salmon, drained, or 1 1/2 cups cooked salmon
- 1 large egg, lightly beaten
- 1 ½ teaspoons Dijon mustard
- 1 3/4 cups fresh whole-wheat breadcrumbs, (see Tip)
- ½ teaspoon freshly ground pepper
- Creamy Dill Sauce (see Associated Recipe)
- 1 lemon, cut into wedges

Calories: 350
Fat: 14g
Carbs: 26g
Protein: 34g

PREPARATION

1. Set oven to 450 degrees Fahrenheit. Coat a large-rimmed baking sheet with cooking spray.
2. In a sizable nonstick skillet over medium-high heat, warm 1 1/2 teaspoons of oil. Add the onion and celery; simmer for about 3 minutes while stirring. After adding the parsley, turn off the heat.
3. In a medium bowl, put the salmon. With a fork, break apart; take off any skin and bones. Stir in the egg and mustard. Mix well after adding the breadcrumbs, onion mixture, and pepper. Create 8 roughly 2 1/2-inch-wide patties out of the mixture.
4. In the pan, heat the remaining 1 1/2 tablespoons of oil. Add 4 patties and cook for 2 to 3 minutes, or until the undersides are brown. Turn them over onto the prepared baking sheet using a wide spatula. The remaining patties should be repeated.
5. Bake the salmon cakes for 15 to 20 minutes, or until they are heated all the way through. Make the Creamy Dill Sauce in the meantime. Serve lemon wedges and sauce alongside the salmon cakes.

SWEET POTATO CARBONARA WITH SPINACH & MUSHROOMS

4 SERVINGS

DIFFICULT

COST

INGREDIENTS

- 2 pounds sweet potatoes, peeled
- 3 large eggs, beaten
- 1 cup grated Parmesan cheese
- ¼ teaspoon salt
- ¼ teaspoon ground pepper
- 1 tablespoon extra-virgin olive oil
- 3 strips center-cut bacon, chopped
- 1 ounce package sliced mushrooms
- 2 cloves garlic, minced
- 1 ounce package baby spinach

Calories: 312
Fat: 12g
Carbs: 38g
Protein: 15g

PREPARATION

1. Start the water in a big pot to boil.
2. Cut sweet potatoes lengthwise into long, thin strands using a spiral vegetable slicer or a julienne vegetable peeler.
3. Cook the sweet potatoes in the boiling water, gently stirring once or twice, for 1 1/2 to 3 minutes, or until they just begin to soften but are still slightly firm. After draining, save 1/4 cup of the cooking water. Off the heat, add the noodles back to the saucepan. In a bowl, whisk the eggs with the Parmesan, salt, pepper, and the conserved water. Pour the mixture over the noodles and toss gently with tongs to coat.
- Heat oil in a large skillet over medium heat. Add bacon and mushrooms and cook, stirring often, until the liquid has evaporated and the mushrooms are starting to brown, 6 to 8 minutes. Add garlic and cook, stirring, until fragrant, about 1 minute.
- Add spinach and cook, stirring, until wilted, 1 to 2 minutes. Add the vegetables to the noodles and toss to combine.
- Top with a generous grinding of pepper

4 SERVINGS

DIFFICULT

COST

CORIANDER-&-LEMON-CRUSTED SALMON
WITH ASPARAGUS SALAD & POACHED EGG

INGREDIENTS

- 1 tablespoon coriander seeds
- 1 teaspoon lemon zest
- ¾ teaspoon fine sea salt, divided
- ½ teaspoon crushed red pepper
- 1 pound wild salmon (see Tips), skin-on, cut into 4 portions
- 1 pound asparagus, trimmed
- 2 tablespoons extra-virgin olive oil
- 1 tablespoon lemon juice
- 1 tablespoon chopped fresh mint
- 1 tablespoon chopped fresh tarragon
- ¼ teaspoon ground pepper, plus more for garnish
- 8 cups water
- 1 tablespoon white vinegar
- 4 large eggs

Calories: 288
Fat: 16g
Carbs: 14g
Protein: 26g

PREPARATION

1. Place a rack in the upper third of the oven and turn the broiler to high. Spray cooking oil on a baking sheet with a rim.
2. For about 3 minutes, while shaking the pan periodically over medium heat, toast the coriander until aromatic. Coriander, lemon zest, 1/2 teaspoon salt, and crushed red pepper should be finely minced in a spice grinder. Place the salmon on the prepared baking sheet after coating the flesh with the spice mixture (approximately 1 1/2 tablespoons each part).
3. Trim asparagus's tips, then slice the stalks diagonally into very thin slices. Toss the tips and slices with the remaining 1/4 teaspoon salt, pepper, mint, lemon juice, and tarragon. While you prepare the eggs and salmon, let stand.
4. In a big pot, bring water and vinegar to a boil.
5. In the meantime, broil the salmon for 3 to 6 minutes, depending on thickness, until just cooked through. To stay warm, make a foil tent.
6. Bring the boiling water to a simmering boil. To get the water to swirl around the saucepan, gently whisk in a circle. Crack eggs into the water one at a time. Cook for 3 to 4 minutes, or until the whites are set but the yolks are still runny.
7. Divide the salmon and asparagus salad among 4 dishes before serving. Create a nest in each salad and place an egg on top.

4 SERVINGS

DIFFICULT

$ COST

HAZELNUT-PARSLEY ROAST TILAPIA

INGREDIENTS

- 2 tablespoons olive oil, divided
- 4 (5 ounce) tilapia fillets (fresh or frozen, thawed)
- ⅓ cup finely chopped hazelnuts
- ¼ cup finely chopped fresh parsley
- 1 small shallot, minced
- 2 teaspoons lemon zest
- ⅛ teaspoon salt plus 1/4 teaspoon, divided
- ¼ teaspoon ground pepper, divided
- 1 ½ tablespoons lemon juice

Calories: 262
Fat: 15g
Carbs: 3g
Protein: 30g

PREPARATION

1. Preheat oven to 450 degrees F. Line a large rimmed baking sheet with foil; brush with 1 Tbsp. oil. Bring fish to room temperature by letting it stand on the counter for 15 minutes.
2. Meanwhile, stir together hazelnuts, parsley, shallot, lemon zest, 1 tsp. oil, 1/8 tsp. salt, and 1/8 tsp. pepper in a small bowl.
3. Pat both sides of the fish dry with a paper towel. Place the fish on the prepared baking sheet. Brush both sides of the fish with lemon juice and the remaining 2 tsp. oil. Season both sides evenly with the remaining 1/4 tsp. salt and 1/8 tsp. pepper. Divide the hazelnut mixture evenly among the tops of the fillets and pat gently to adhere.
4. Roast the fish until it is opaque, firm, and just beginning to flake, 7 to 10 minutes. Serve immediately.

6 SERVINGS

DIFFICULT

$ **COST**

MIXED VEGETABLE SALAD WITH LIME DRESSING

INGREDIENTS

- ¼ cup canola oil
- ¼ cup extra-virgin olive oil
- 3 tablespoons lime juice
- 1 ½ tablespoons finely chopped fresh cilantro
- ½ teaspoon salt
- ½ teaspoon ground pepper
- 2 cups mixed vegetables (steamed: sliced small red potatoes, carrots or beets, green beans, peas; raw: sliced radishes, cucumbers or tomatoes)
- 6 leaves romaine or leaf lettuce
- 1 small bunch watercress, large stems removed
- 1 hard-boiled large egg, sliced
- 1 thick slice red onion, broken into rings
- Crumbled Mexican queso fresco, feta or farmer's cheese for garnish

PREPARATION

1. In a medium bowl, stir together the canola and olive oils, lime juice, cilantro, salt, and pepper. A mixture of vegetables is added; toss to combine.

2. Line a large serving platter with lettuce. Place a serving dish on top of the prepared veggies. If preferred, top with egg, onion, and cheese after surrounding with watercress.

NOTES

Calories: 214
Fat: 2g
Carbs: 28g
Protein: 6g

Snacks

24 SERVINGS

DIFFICULT

COST

APRICOT-SUNFLOWER GRANOLA BARS

INGREDIENTS

- 3 cups old-fashioned rolled oats
- 1 cup crispy brown rice cereal
- 1 cup finely chopped dried apricots (1/4 inch)
- ½ cup unsalted pepitas, toasted
- ½ cup unsalted sunflower seeds, toasted
- ¼ teaspoon salt
- ⅔ cup brown rice syrup or light corn syrup
- ½ cup sunflower seed butter
- 1 teaspoon ground cinnamon

Calories: 152
Fat: 6g
Carbs: 22g
Protein: 4g

PREPARATION

1. Set oven to 325 degrees Fahrenheit. Put parchment paper on the bottom and edges of a 9 by 13-inch baking pan, leaving some hanging over the sides. Spray some cooking spray on the parchment paper lightly.
2. In a sizable bowl, mix the oats, rice cereal, pepitas, sunflower seeds, and salt.
3. In a bowl that can be heated in the microwave, mix rice syrup (or corn syrup), sunflower butter, and cinnamon. 30 seconds in the microwave (or 1 minute in a saucepan over medium heat). Stir to incorporate the addition with the dry ingredients. Use the back of a spatula to transfer to the prepared pan and press firmly into the pan.
4. For chewier bars, bake for 20 to 25 minutes, or until the edges are just beginning to color but the center is still soft. Bake for 30 to 35 minutes, or until the edges are golden brown and the centers are still somewhat gooey for crunchier bars. (Both remain soft when warm and become firmer as they cool.)
5. For easier lifting out of the pan onto a chopping board (it will still be soft), let cool in the pan for 10 minutes. Cut into 24 bars, then allow to chill for a further 30 minutes without separating the bars. After cooling, cut into bars.

TRADITIONAL GREEK TAHINI DIP

8 SERVINGS

DIFFICULT

$ COST

INGREDIENTS

- ½ cup tahini
- 2 tablespoons lemon juice
- 1 tablespoon extra-virgin olive oil, plus more for garnish
- 1 clove garlic, crushed
- ¼ teaspoon salt
- 6 tablespoons water
- 3 tablespoons chopped fresh parsley
- Toasted sesame seeds for garnish

PREPARATION

1. Salt, garlic, oil, tahini, and lemon juice should all be combined in a food processor. As you pulse, scrape the sides as necessary to ensure smoothness.
2. Add water in a small stream while the motor is running until the mixture is smooth and light in color.
3. Place the dip in a bowl for serving and garnish with parsley.
4. Sesame seeds and more oil may be used as a garnish.

NOTE.

Calories: 106
Fat: 10g
Carbs: 9g
Protein: 3g

CHERRY-COCOA-PISTACHIO ENERGY BALLS

20 SERVINGS

DIFFICULT

COST

INGREDIENTS

- 1 ½ cups dried cherries
- ¾ cup shelled salted pistachios
- ½ cup almond butter
- 3 tablespoons cocoa powder
- 4 tablespoons pure maple syrup
- ½ teaspoon ground cinnamon

PREPARATION

1. In a food processor, mash cherries, pistachios, almond butter, cocoa powder, maple syrup, and cinnamon.
2. When the mixture is crumbly but can be squeezed into a cohesive ball, process for 10 to 20 pulses to finely chop the ingredients. After that, process for about a minute, scraping down the sides as needed.
3. ·Squeeze about 1 tablespoon of the mixture firmly between your palms, then roll into a ball with wet hands (to stop the mixture from clinging to them). Place in a box for storage. The remaining mixture

NOTES

Calories: 72
Fat: 4g
Carbs: 9g
Protein: 2g

AIR-FRYER SWEET POTATO CHIPS

8 SERVINGS

DIFFICULT

$ COST

INGREDIENTS

- 1 medium sweet potato, (about 8 ounces), sliced into 1/8-inch-thick rounds
- 1 tablespoon canola oil
- ¼ teaspoon sea salt
- ¼ teaspoon ground pepper

Calories: 123
Fat: 10g
Carbs: 19g
Protein: 11g

PREPARATION

1. Slices of sweet potato should be soaked for 20 minutes in a big bowl of cold water. Using paper towels, wipe the drain and dry.
2. Sweet potatoes should be put back in the dried dish. Salt, pepper, and oil to taste; gently toss to coat.
3. Spray some cooking spray on the air fryer basket lightly. Just enough sweet potatoes should be arranged in the basket to create one layer.
4. Cook for 15 minutes at 350 degrees F, rotating and rearranging into a single layer every 5 minutes, until well cooked and crispy. Carefully transfer the chips from the air fryer to a platter using tongs. The remaining sweet potatoes should be repeated.
5. Serve the chips right away, or let them cool fully and store them in an airtight plastic container for up to three days. Let the chips cool for five minutes.

4 SERVINGS

DIFFICULT

$ **COST**

TUNA SALAD SPREAD

INGREDIENTS

- 1 avocado, mashed
- 2 tablespoons low-fat plain Greek yogurt
- 1 tablespoon lemon juice
- 1 tablespoon chopped fresh parsley
- ¼ teaspoon garlic powder
- ¼ teaspoon paprika
- ¼ teaspoon salt
- ¼ teaspoon ground pepper
- 1 (5 ounce) can albacore tuna in water, drained
- ¼ cup diced onion or celery

PREPARATION

1. In a small bowl, combine the avocado and yogurt and whisk well. Stir in the parsley, garlic powder, paprika, salt, and pepper after adding the lemon juice.
2. Mix gently until mixed after adding the tuna and onion (or celery).

NOTES

Calories: 130
Fat: 8g
Carbs: 6g
Protein: 10g

4 SERVINGS

DIFFICULT

$ COST

KALE CHIPS

INGREDIENTS

- 1 large bunch kale, tough stems removed, leaves torn into pieces (about 16 cups)
- 1 tablespoon extra-virgin olive oil
- ¼ teaspoon salt

PREPARATION

1. Oven racks should be placed in the upper third and the center.
2. If the kale is moist, completely pat it dry with a clean dishtowel before transferring it to a large bowl. Salt and oil should be drizzled over the kale. To uniformly distribute the oil and salt on the kale leaves, knead them with your hands. Make careful to evenly distribute the kale leaves on 2 big rimmed baking pans. Make the chips in batches if all of the kale will not fit.
3. Bake for 8 to 12 minutes, rotating the pans from front to back and top to bottom halfway through, until the majority of the leaves are crisp. (If only using one baking sheet, check after 8 minutes to avoid scorching.)

 NOTE.

Calories: 110
Fat: 5g
Carbs: 16g
Protein: 5g

24 SERVINGS

DIFFICULT

$ COST

VEGAN CHOCOLATE-DIPPED FROZEN BANANA BITES

INGREDIENTS

- 3 large bananas
- ¼ cup natural peanut butter (chunky or smooth)
- ¾ cup vegan chocolate chips

PREPARATION

1. Each peeled banana should be split lengthwise. Spread peanut butter on each half. Combine the banana halves to create banana "sandwiches." From each banana "sandwich," cut 8 rounds. Place the frozen banana pieces on a baking sheet or tray that has been lined with parchment paper or wax paper, and freeze for at least two hours or overnight.

2. Place chocolate chips in a microwave-safe bowl and microwave on High, in 15-second increments, until melted (1 to 1 1/2 minutes total). Each frozen banana bite is coated with chocolate on one half.

3. Let the chocolate stand until it has hardened. If not serving right away, put the food back in the freezer.

NOTES

Calories: 58
Fat: 3g
Carbs: 8g
Protein: 1g

FRUIT ENERGY BALLS

24 SERVINGS

DIFFICULT

COST

INGREDIENTS

- 1 cup chopped almonds
- 1 cup dried figs
- 1 cup dried apricots
- ⅓ cup unsweetened shredded coconut

PREPARATION

1. Combine almonds, figs and apricots in a food processor; pulse until finely chopped.
2. Roll the mixture into small balls and dredge in coconut

 NOTES

Calories: 70
Fat: 3g
Carbs: 10g
Protein: 2g

10 SERVINGS

DIFFICULT

COST

ROASTED BEET HUMMUS

INGREDIENTS

- 1 (15 ounce) can no-salt-added chickpeas, rinsed
- 8 ounces roasted beets, coarsely chopped and patted dry
- ¼ cup tahini
- ¼ cup extra-virgin olive oil
- ¼ cup lemon juice
- 1 clove garlic
- 1 teaspoon ground cumin
- ½ teaspoon salt

PREPARATION

1. In a food processor, combine chickpeas, beets, tahini, oil, lemon juice, garlic, cumin, and salt.
2. Puree for 2 to 3 minutes, or until very smooth. Serve with crudités, pita chips, or vegetable chips.

 NOTES

Calories: 133
Fat: 10g
Carbs: 10g
Protein: 3g

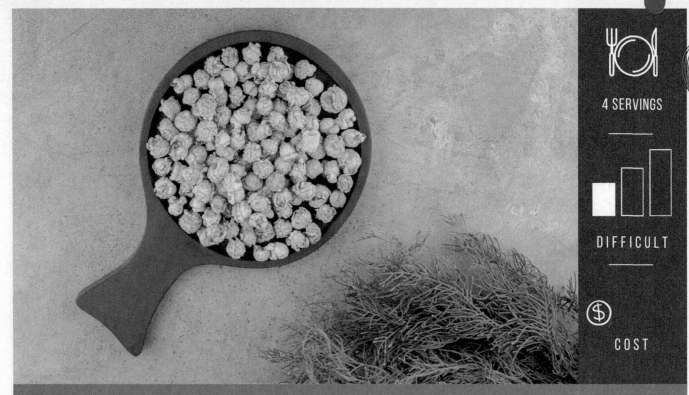

AIR-FRYER CRISPY CHICKPEAS

INGREDIENTS

- 1 (15 ounce) can unsalted chickpeas, rinsed and drained
- 1 ½ tablespoons toasted sesame oil
- ¼ teaspoon smoked paprika
- ¼ teaspoon crushed red pepper
- ⅛ teaspoon salt
- Cooking spray
- 2 lime wedges

PREPARATION

1. On multiple layers of paper towels, spread the chickpeas. Roll the chickpeas beneath the paper towels to dry them on all sides, then add additional paper towels on top and pat until extremely dry.
2. Combine the chickpeas and oil in a medium bowl. Salt, crushed red pepper, and paprika should be added.
3. Pour into a cooking spray-coated air fryer basket. Cook for 12 to 14 minutes at 400 degrees F, shaking the basket occasionally, until very nicely browned.
4. Serve the chickpeas with lime wedges on top.

NOTE

Calories: 132
Fat: 6g
Carbs: 14g
Protein: 5g

5 SERVINGS

DIFFICULT

$

COST

HOMEMADE TRAIL MIX

INGREDIENTS

- ¼ cup whole shelled (unpeeled) almonds
- ¼ cup unsalted dry-roasted peanuts
- ¼ cup dried cranberries
- ¼ cup chopped pitted dates
- 2 ounces dried apricots, or other dried fruit

PREPARATION

1. Combine almonds, peanuts, cranberries, dates and apricots (or other fruit) in a medium bowl.

NOTES

Calories: 132
Fat: 7g
Carbs: 15g
Protein: 4g

ROASTED BUFFALO CHICKPEAS

4 SERVINGS

DIFFICULT

COST

INGREDIENTS

- 1 tablespoon white vinegar
- ½ teaspoon cayenne pepper, or to taste
- ¼ teaspoon salt
- 1 (15 ounce) can no-salt-added chickpeas, rinsed

PREPARATION

1. Oven rack should be in the upper third; heat to 400 degrees F.
2. Salt, cayenne, and vinegar are combined in a sizable basin. Chickpeas should be dried very completely before being mixed with the vinegar mixture.
3. Spread on a baking sheet with a rim. For 30 to 35 minutes, roast the chickpeas, tossing twice, until they are crisp and golden. The chickpeas will become crisp as they cool; leave to cool for 30 minutes on the pan.

 NOTES

Calories: 109
Fat: 1g
Carbs: 18g
Protein: 6g

10 SERVINGS

DIFFICULT

$ **COST**

AVOCADO HUMMUS

INGREDIENTS

- 1 (15 ounce) can no-salt-added chickpeas
- 1 ripe avocado, halved and pitted
- 1 cup fresh cilantro leaves
- ¼ cup tahini
- ¼ cup extra-virgin olive oil
- ¼ cup lemon juice
- 1 clove garlic
- 1 teaspoon ground cumin
- ½ teaspoon salt

Calories: 156
Fat: 12g
Carbs: 10g
Protein: 3g

PREPARATION

1. Chickpeas should be drained, with 2 tablespoons of the liquid saved.
2. Add the chickpeas and the liquid you set aside to a food processor. Avocado, cilantro, tahini, oil, lemon juice, garlic, cumin, and salt should all be added. until very smooth, puree.
3. Serve with crudités, pita chips, or vegetable chips.

 **NOTES**

BEET CHIPS

5 SERVINGS

DIFFICULT

COST

INGREDIENTS

- 2 large beets (about 1 pound), thinly sliced (about 1/8 inch thick)
- 1 tablespoon extra-virgin olive oil
- ½ teaspoon salt

PREPARATION

1. Oven to 200 degrees Fahrenheit. 2 big baking sheets should be lined with parchment paper.
2. Slices of beet are tossed with salt and oil. Place on the preheated baking sheets in a single layer.
3. Bake for about three hours, turning the pans top to bottom and front to back, on the upper and lower oven racks, until crisp. Before serving, let the pans cool for 30 minutes.

 NOTE.

Calories: 33
Fat: 2g
Carbs: 13g
Protein: 3g

15 SERVINGS

DIFFICULT

$ COST

BANANA ENERGY BITES

INGREDIENTS

- 1 overripe banana
- 1 cup dry quick-cooking rolled oats
- ½ cup roasted and salted pumpkin seeds (pepitas)
- ½ cup dried cranberries
- ½ cup natural peanut butter
- ¼ cup miniature semisweet chocolate pieces

PREPARATION

1. With a fork, mash the banana in a medium bowl until it is smooth. Oats, pumpkin seeds, dried cranberries, peanut butter, and chocolate chunks should all be stirred in.
2. Shape the mixture into 32 balls, using 1 tbsp for each bite; gently flatten.
3. Up to serving time, chill.

 NOTES

Calories: 145
Fat: 9g
Carbs: 14g
Protein: 5g

Dessert

WINE-POACHED PEARS

INGREDIENTS

- 2 cups dry red wine (such as Cabernet, Pinot Noir, or Merlot)
- 5 tablespoons sugar
- 1/2 cup orange juice
- 1 to 2 tablespoons orange zest
- 1 cinnamon stick
- 2 whole cloves
- 4 firm, ripe pears, free of blemishes, peeled, stems intact
- Vanilla Greek yogurt (optional)
- Toasted almond slices (optional)
- Fresh mint (optional)

PREPARATION

1. Wine, sugar, orange juice, orange zest, cinnamon stick, and cloves should all be combined in a 4-quart saucepan. Stir the sugar until it melts.
2. Bring the liquid to a boil before adding the pears. Once the pears are uniformly colored and soft, simmer them for 15 to 20 minutes with the lid on, turning them every five minutes.
3. The peaches should be placed in a dish to cool. After removing the cinnamon and cloves, boil the liquid for another 15 to 20 minutes, or until it has thickened and reduced by half.
4. A few teaspoons of the warm syrup should be drizzled over the pears when they are ready to be served, whether warm or at room temperature. If desired, garnish with a dollop of Greek yogurt, sliced almonds, and fresh mint.

Calories: 245
Fat: 2g
Carbs: 44g
Protein: 6g

STRAWBERRIES WITH PEPPERED BALSAMIC DRIZZLE

INGREDIENTS

- 2 cups fresh strawberries, washed and cut in half
- 1 tablespoon balsamic vinegar
- 1 tablespoon brown sugar
- Pinch freshly and finely ground black pepper
- 4 ounces vanilla Greek yogurt
- Fresh mint, for garnish

PREPARATION

1. Strawberries, balsamic vinegar, sugar, and pepper should all be combined in a bowl. To make sure the berries are evenly coated, gently stir. For one hour, cover and leave at room temperature; after that, chill until ready to serve.
2. Add a dollop of yogurt on top after evenly distributing the strawberries across the four dishes.
3. Serve after adding a fresh mint leaf to the garnish.

 NOTE.

Calories: 65
Fat: 2g
Carbs: 16g
Protein: 6g

10 SERVINGS

DIFFICULT

$ COST

VANILLA CHIA SEED PUDDING WITH TOPPINGS

INGREDIENTS

- 1 cup vanilla Greek yogurt
- 2 cups reduced-fat 2 percent milk
- 1/2 cup chia seeds
- 1-1/2 tablespoons maple syrup
- 1/2 teaspoon vanilla extract
- Pinch salt

PREPARATION

1. Whisk the yogurt, milk, chia seeds, maple syrup, vanilla, and salt until well combined in a large bowl.
2. Overnight or for three to four hours, cover and chill. If necessary, whisk the mixture one more just before serving to remove any clumps that may have developed.
3. Place in dessert cups and decorate with your preferred garnishes.

 NOTES

Calories: 92
Fat: 4g
Carbs: 10g
Protein: 6g

MANGO BANANA SOFT SERVE

6 SERVINGS

DIFFICULT

COST

INGREDIENTS

- 1 large ripe banana
- One 16-ounce package frozen mango chunks
- 1 to 2 tablespoons sugar
- 1-1/2 tablespoons lime juice
- 1-1/2 tablespoons canned light coconut milk
- Mint leaves, for garnish

PREPARATION

1. Bananas should be peeled, sliced in half, placed in a freezer bag that can be sealed, and frozen for at least four hours or until solid.
2. Mango and sugar should be combined in a sizable basin and left to stand for 5 minutes. (Skip the sugar if you'd like a little more acidity.)
3. Use the tamper to scrape down the sides of the high-speed blender as you pulse the mango, banana, lime juice, and coconut milk for 3 to 4 minutes, or until the mixture is thick and smooth.
4. For a softer consistency, scoop the soft serve into bowls and serve right away; otherwise, freeze until ready to serve. If desired, add mint leaves as a garnish.

NOTES

Calories: 92
Fat: 4g
Carbs: 21g
Protein: 6g

°F	°C
50	10
100	37
150	65
200	93
250	121
300	150
350	176
400	204
450	232

US	EU
1 teaspoon	5 gr
1 tablespoon	15 gr
1 cup	250 gr
1/2 cup	125 gr
1 oz	30 gr
10 oz	315 gr
1 pound	16 oz/454 gr
1 cup	16 tablespoon
1 tablespoon	3 teaspoon

30 DAYS MEAL PLAN

WEEK 1

Monday

Berry-Almond Smoothie Bowl	BREAKFAST PG. 39
Veggie & Hummus Sandwich	LUNCH PG. 56
Smoked Salmon Salad Nicoise	DINNER PG. 58
Kale Chips	EXTRA PG. 96

Tuesday

Spinach-Avocado Smoothie	BREAKFAST PG. 53
Spinach & Strawberry Meal-Prep Salad	LUNCH PG. 57
Sweet Potato, Kale & Chicken Salad	DINNER PG. 59
Fruit Energy Balls	EXTRA PG. 98

Wednesday

Cantaloupe Smoothie	BREAKFAST PG. 52
Smoked Salmon Salad Nicoise	LUNCH PG. 58
Meal-Prep Vegan Lettuce Wraps	DINNER PG. 60
Roasted Beet Hummus	EXTRA PG. 99

Thursday

Vegan Smoothie Bowl	BREAKFAST PG. 50
Winter Kale & Quinoa Salad with Avocado	LUNCH PG. 62
Slow-Cooker Chicken Soup	DINNER PG. 64
Air-Fryer Crispy Chickpeas	EXTRA PG. 100

Friday

White Bean & Avocado Toast	BREAKFAST PG. 49
Roasted Root Vegetables...	LUNCH PG. 65
Winter Kale & Quinoa Salad with Avocado	DINNER PG. 62
Avocado Hummus	EXTRA PG. 103

Saturday

Mango-Ginger Smoothie	BREAKFAST PG. 48
Eggplant Parmesan	LUNCH PG. 66
Chicken & Vegetable Penne	DINNER PG. 70
Homemade Trail Mix	EXTRA PG. 101

Sunday

Peanut Butter Banana Toast	BREAKFAST PG. 51
Chicken & Vegetable penne...	LUNCH PG. 70
Dijon Salmon with Green Bean Pilaf	DINNER PG. 73
Roasted Buffalo Chickpeas	EXTRA PG. 102

Notes

THIS IS A SUGGESTION ON HOW TO COMBINE MEALS, CREATE YOUR OWN PLAN TOO...

WEEK 2

Monday

Chocolate-Banana
Protein Smoothie
BREAKFAST
PG. 42

Sweet Potato, Kale
& Chicken Salad
LUNCH
PG. 59

Smoked Salmon
Salad Nicoise
DINNER
PG. 58

Air-Fryer Sweet
Potato Chips
EXTRA
PG. 94

Tuesday

Raspberry Yogurt
Cereal Bowl
BREAKFAST
PG. 43

Mason Jar Power Salad
LUNCH
PG. 61

Creamy Lemon
Pasta with Shrimp
DINNER
PG. 75

Vegan Chocolate
Dipped Frozen
Banana Bites
EXTRA
PG. 97

Wednesday

Spinach & Egg Tacos
BREAKFAST
PG. 44

Walnut-Rosemary
Crusted Salmon
LUNCH
PG. 68

Slow-Cooker
Vegetarian Bolognese
DINNER
PG. 77

Strawberries with
Peppered Balsamic
Drizzle
EXTRA
PG. 108

Thursday

White Bean
& Avocado Toast
BREAKFAST
PG. 49

Hasselback Eggplant
Parmesan
LUNCH
PG. 69

Slow-Cooker
Chicken Soup
DINNER
PG. 64

Mango Banana
Soft Serve
EXTRA
PG. 110

Friday

Sheet-pan Chicken
with Roasted...
BREAKFAST
PG. 71

Roasted Root
Vegetables...
LUNCH
PG. 65

Salmon
Couscous Salad
DINNER
PG. 78

Vanilla Chia Seed
Pudding with Toppings
EXTRA
PG. 109

Saturday

Spinach-Avocado
Smoothie
BREAKFAST
PG. 53

Chicken Caesar
Pasta Salad
LUNCH
PG. 72

Slow-Cooker Chicken
& Orzo...
DINNER
PG. 80

Wine-Poached Pears
EXTRA
PG. 107

Sunday

Vegan Smoothie
Bowl
BREAKFAST
PG. 50

Slow-Cooker
Vegetarian Bolognese
LUNCH
PG. 74

Fig & Goat
Cheese Salad
DINNER
PG. 83

Homemade Trail Mix
EXTRA
PG. 101

Notes

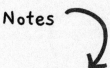

WEEK 3

Monday

BREAKFAST
Pineapple Green Smoothie — PG. 41

LUNCH
Spinach & Strawberry Meal-Prep Salad — PG. 57

DINNER
Eggplant Parmesan — PG. 66

EXTRA
Kale Chips — PG. 96

Tuesday

BREAKFAST
Chocolate-Banana Protein Smoothie — PG. 42

LUNCH
Mason Jar Power Salad — PG. 61

DINNER
Chicken-Quinoa Bowl with Olives & Cucumber — PG. 67

EXTRA
Vegan Chocolate Dipped Frozen Banana Bites — PG. 97

Wednesday

BREAKFAST
Fruit & Yogurt Smoothie — PG. 46

LUNCH
Smoked Salmon Salad Nicoise — PG. 58

DINNER
Slow-Cooker Vegetarian Bolognese — PG. 77

EXTRA
Air-Fryer Crispy Chickpeas — PG. 100

Thursday

BREAKFAST
White Bean & Avocado Toast — PG. 49

LUNCH
Meal-Prep Vegan Lettuce Wraps — PG. 60

DINNER
Chicken Caesar Pasta Salad — PG. 72

EXTRA
Beet Chips — PG. 104

Friday

BREAKFAST
Vegan Smoothie Bowl — PG. 50

LUNCH
Salad with Chickpeas & Tuna — PG. 61

DINNER
Slow-Cooker Vegetarian Bolognese — PG. 74

EXTRA
Wine-Poached Pears — PG. 107

Saturday

BREAKFAST
Vegan Smoothie Bowl — PG. 50

LUNCH
Vegan Superfood Grain Bowls — PG. 63

DINNER
Creamy Lemon Pasta with Shrimp — PG. 75

EXTRA
Roasted Beet Hummus — PG. 99

Sunday

BREAKFAST
Peanut Butter-Banana Cinnamon Toast — PG. 51

LUNCH
Slow-Cooker Chicken & Chickpea Soup — PG. 64

DINNER
Dijon Salmon with Green Bean Pilaf — PG. 73

EXTRA
Homemade Trail Mix — PG. 101

Notes

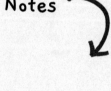

WEEK 4

Monday

Meal-Prep Vegan Lettuce Wraps	BREAKFAST PG. 60
Cauliflower Taco Bowls	LUNCH PG. 55
Salmon & Asparagus	DINNER PG. 81
Kale Chips	EXTRA PG. 96

Tuesday

Spinach & Egg Scramble	BREAKFAST PG. 40
Smoked Salmon Salad Nicoise	LUNCH PG. 58
	DINNER PG. 84
Wine-Poached Pears	EXTRA PG. 107

Wednesday

Spinach & Egg Tacos	BREAKFAST PG. 44
Smoked Salmon Salad Nicoise	LUNCH PG. 58
Carbonara with Spinach & Mushrooms	DINNER PG. 86
Beet Chips	EXTRA PG. 104

Thursday

Really Green Smoothie	BREAKFAST PG. 45
Veggie & Hummus Sandwich	LUNCH PG. 56
Fig & Goat Cheese Salad	DINNER PG. 83
Banana Energy Bites	EXTRA PG. 105

Friday

Fruit & Yogurt Smoothie	BREAKFAST PG. 46
Cauliflower Taco Bowls	LUNCH PG. 55
Easy Salmon Cakes	DINNER PG. 85
Roasted Buffalo Chickpeas	EXTRA PG. 102

Saturday

Mango-Ginger Smoothie	BREAKFAST PG. 48
Vegan Superfood Grain Bowls	LUNCH PG. 63
Carbonara with Spinach & Mushrooms	DINNER PG. 86
Air-Fryer Crispy Chickpeas	EXTRA PG. 100

Sunday

Vegan Smoothie Bowl	BREAKFAST PG. 50
Vegan Superfood Grain Bowls	LUNCH PG. 63
Salmon with Asparagus	DINNER PG. 87
Strawberries with Peppered Balsamic Drizzle	EXTRA PG. 108

Notes

WEEK 5

Monday

Fruit & Yogurt Smoothie	BREAKFAST PG. 46
Cauliflower Taco Bowls	LUNCH PG. 55
Fig & Goat Cheese Salad	DINNER PG. 83
Kale Chips	EXTRA PG. 96

Tuesday

Really Green Smoothie	BREAKFAST PG. 45
Vegan Superfood Grain Bowls	LUNCH PG. 63
Chicken Pesto Pasta with Asparagus	DINNER PG. 84
Air-Fryer Crispy Chickpeas	EXTRA PG. 100

Wednesday

Vegan Smoothie Bowl	BREAKFAST PG. 50
Vegan Superfood Grain Bowls	LUNCH PG. 63
Carbonara with Spinach & Mushrooms	DINNER PG. 86
Beet Chips	EXTRA PG. 104

Thursday

Mango-Ginger Smoothie	BREAKFAST PG. 48
Veggie & Hummus Sandwich	LUNCH PG. 56
Easy Salmon Cakes	DINNER PG. 85
Wine-Poached Pears	EXTRA PG. 107

Friday

Meal-Prep Vegan Lettuce Wraps	BREAKFAST PG. 60
Smoked Salmon Salad Nicoise	LUNCH PG. 58
Salmon with Asparagus	DINNER PG. 87
Strawberries with Peppered Balsamic Drizzle	EXTRA PG. 108

Saturday

Spinach & Egg Tacos	BREAKFAST PG. 44
Cauliflower Taco Bowls	LUNCH PG. 55
Carbonara with Spinach & Mushrooms	DINNER PG. 86
Banana Energy Bites	EXTRA PG. 105

Sunday

Spinach & Egg Scramble	BREAKFAST PG. 40
Smoked Salmon Salad Nicoise	LUNCH PG. 58
Salmon & Asparagus	DINNER PG. 81
Roasted Buffalo Chickpeas	EXTRA PG. 102

Notes

Hi, I'm Robert

12/11/1972
Zodiac Sign, Scorpio
Height, 181 cm

Who am I ?

Robert is a journalist passionate about nutrition, diet, and exercise. From a young age, he has shown a keen interest in health and wellness, recognizing the importance of a balanced diet and an active lifestyle.

After obtaining a degree in journalism, Robert decided to specialize in the field of nutrition and fitness. He began studying various dietary theories and exploring the most effective approaches to maintaining a healthy lifestyle. During his educational journey, he learned the fundamentals of food science and developed a deep understanding of how food affects the body and mind.

With a solid knowledge base, Robert started writing articles on diets, nutrition, and training for various magazines and websites. He worked with industry experts and interviewed renowned nutritionists, dieticians, and personal trainers to gain a broader perspective on best practices in this field.

Robert's mission is to educate the public about adopting a healthy approach to nutrition and exercise. He believes that good nutrition is essential for achieving a balanced life and that regular physical activity is crucial for long-term well-being.

In addition to writing informative articles, Robert conducts in-depth research on diets and emerging food trends. He constantly seeks to stay updated on the latest scientific discoveries in the field of nutrition and exercise, in order to provide accurate, evidence-based information to his readers.

Robert's passion for nutrition and fitness extends to his personal life as well. He follows a balanced diet and regularly engages in physical activities to maintain fitness and overall well-being. He firmly believes that adopting a healthy lifestyle is an investment in one's future, bringing benefits not only physically but also mentally and emotionally.

Through his work, Robert aims to inspire others to take care of their health through mindful food choices and adequate physical activity. His hope is that the information he shares can help people improve their lives and achieve long-term wellness.

HEALTHY EATING

TAKE REGULAR EXERCISE

GOOD RELATIONSHIPS

LIVE BETTER AND LONGER

MEAL JOURNAL

A weight loss journal, a valuable tool for documenting and tracking weight loss progress, serves as an individual's personal log to record food intake, exercise routines, and lifestyle habits. By meticulously noting details like meals, calorie counts, portion sizes, exercise duration, and any other relevant factors, the journal provides a comprehensive overview of one's commitment to achieving a healthy weight.

FOOD LABELS

Understanding nutritional content, ingredients, and sourcing empowers us to make healthy decisions that align with our needs. Transparency in the food industry and support for sustainable practices are also benefits. Make informed choices, promote better health, and support a healthier food environment.

DASH DIET RECIPES FOR SPECIAL OCCASIONS

Dish up delicious DASH-friendly meals that are perfect for any celebration, without compromising your health goals.

SUPER BONUS: MEDITERRANEAN DIET COOKBOOK

FULL DIGITAL VERSION!

Did you like the DASH DIET COOKBOOK?

Let me know, scan the QR code

and leave a review on Amazon.

It will take you less than a minute, but it's very important to me.

THANK YOU!

Notes

Printed in Great Britain
by Amazon

40299638R00071